A POCKET GUIDE TO . . .

Social Issues

What does the Bible say about morality?

1:1
answersingenesis
Petersburg, Kentucky, USA

Copyright ©2009 Answers in Genesis–USA. All rights reserved. No part of this book may be used or reproduced in any manner whatsoever without written permission from the publisher. For more information write: Answers in Genesis, PO Box 510, Hebron, KY 41048

Sixth printing: December 2011

ISBN: 1-60092-262-7

All Scripture quotations are taken from the New King James Version. Copyright ©1982 by Thomas Nelson, Inc. Used by permission. All rights reserved.

Printed in China

www.answersingenesis.org

Table of Contents

Introduction

America is in the middle of a culture war. The battle lines are drawn around issues that polarize our society. There are many labels that get attached to these ideas, but labels can often be misleading. In order to understand the issues, it is important to look at them from both sides. The biblical side of these issues is not well-represented in the media. In the following chapters, the biblical perspective will be laid out alongside the secular understanding of the issues.

While most people would consider themselves moral, why is morality a good thing? Who gets to decide what is right and wrong? Without an ultimate standard, what is right or wrong can change. Murder may be wrong in America today and legal in a few years—if the majority votes for it. Understanding who should decide what is right and wrong is a fundamental part of understanding the culture wars.

What does the Bible teach when it comes to the different races? How does an understanding of the beginning of life relate to the abortion and cloning issues? Should man clone animals and plants to help feed the hungry? Should the size, condition, or location of a person make it legal to take his or her life? These questions and others will be answered from an authoritative source—the Bible.

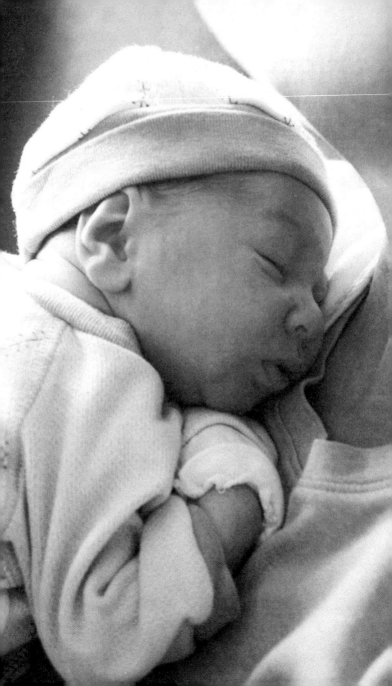

When Does Life Begin?

by Tommy Mitchell

When does human life begin? This question has confounded individuals and divided our society. Opinions have come from the right and the left, from pro-life advocates and those in favor of abortion on demand, from physicians and lawyers, from the pulpit and the courtroom.

When did I begin to be me? Is this a scientific question or a theological one?[1] Would this question be best left to scientists or to preachers and philosophers? Information and viewpoints from secular scientific sources and from theologians will be examined in this chapter, but the ultimate answer can have no authority unless that answer is based squarely on the Word of God. The Bible, because it is true, will not disagree with genuine science. Furthermore, the Bible is the only valid and consistent basis for making moral judgments, since it comes from the Creator of the whole world and all people in it. Any other basis for judgment would be a useless clamor of divergent, man-made opinions.

Who is more human?

Life is a continuum. From the season of growing in the womb to being born, from playing as a child to growing older, each stage of life seems to blend gracefully (or not so gracefully in my case) into the next. Life progresses and time passes, culminating in death. Death, a very visible end point, is more easily defined than the point at which the continuum of human life begins.

Where is the starting point? If life is indeed a continual process, can we not just work backward to its beginning? There are a variety of opinions about life's beginnings. Many say life begins at conception. Others argue strongly that life does not start until implantation in the womb. Still others say that human life begins only when the umbilical cord is cut, making the newborn child an independent agent. How is fact separated from opinion?

Perhaps another way to ask the question is, when do we become human? Certainly a child sitting on grandpa's knee or a fully grown adult would be considered human. Is the adult *more* human than the child? Of course not. No reasonable person would consider the child to be less human. At what point along the journey did this child become human? Was it at conception, somewhere during his development, or at birth?

The process

The initial event along the road of human development is fertilization. Twenty-three chromosomes from the mother and 23 chromosomes from the father are combined at the time of fertilization. At this point, the genetic makeup of the individual is determined. At this time, a unique individual, known as a *zygote*, begins to exist. But is this zygote human?

This zygote then divides again and again. Some cells develop into the placenta and are essential for implantation. Other cells develop into the anatomical parts of the baby.[2] The number of cells increases rapidly, and the name changes as the number increases. By the time this rapidly dividing ball of cells arrives in the uterus, it is called a *blastocyst*. Implantation in the uterine wall normally occurs about six days after fertilization.[3]

For reasons unclear to medical science, the mass of cells sometimes splits to produce identical twins. These twins are called identical because their sets of chromosomes are identical. Depending upon the stage of development when the split occurs, the twins may share certain placental parts, but the twins produced are distinct individuals. If the split occurs between the 13th and 15th days, the twins will actually share body parts, a condition known as *conjoined twins*, commonly called *Siamese twins*. (After that time, development and differentiation are too far along to allow successful splitting.)

Even though the names arbitrarily change throughout this process and certain milestones in development are evident, the process set in motion at the moment of conception is a continuous chain of events. In this sequence, groups of cells multiply and develop into specific body parts with amazing precision and a remarkably low rate of error, considering the complexity of changes that must occur. However, at no time in this process is there a scientific point at which the developing individual clearly "becomes a person," any more than a baby becomes more human when it walks, talks, or is weaned. These milestones in zygote, blastocyst, embryonic, and fetal development are simply descriptions of anatomy, not hurdles met in the test of humanness. From a scientific point of view, the words are arbitrary and purely descriptive.

Can science help?

Scientists have studied the marvelous process previously described for decades. The changes in the form of the embryo through each stage are well documented. The question still remains, at what point does human life begin? There are numerous positions on this. Some of these will be reviewed here.

A genetic position

The simplest view is based on genetics. Those who hold this position argue that since a genetically unique individual is created at the time of fertilization, each human life begins at fertilization. The zygote formed at fertilization is different from all others and, if it survives, will grow into a person with his or her own unique set of genes. In this view, the terms *fertilization* and *conception* are interchangeable. Thus, in this view, life would be said to begin at conception.

The phenomenon of twinning is sometimes used to argue against this position. Until about day 14, there is the possibility that the zygote will split, producing twins. Those who oppose a genetic view say that there is no uniqueness to the zygote, no humanness or personhood, until the potential for twinning has passed. They ask, if the zygote is an individual "person" at fertilization, then what is the nature of that "personhood" if the zygote should split into two individuals?

Another objection to this view is the fact the many fertilized eggs never successfully implant. An estimated 20–50 percent of fertilizations die or are spontaneously aborted.[4] Thus, those who raise this objection hold that, since there are such a large number of zygotes that never fully develop, those zygotes are not truly human.

However, neither of the objections can be so easily supported. The twinning objection falls short when one considers the problem presented by the existence of so-called Siamese twins. In these cases, the zygote does not completely split, and the children are born joined together, often sharing certain body organs. Nonetheless, both twins have distinct personalities and are distinct individuals. Here the "personhood" obviously could not be granted after twinning since the process was never completed.

The second objection, the high loss rate of zygotes, is also not logical. The occurrence of spontaneous abortions does not mean that the lost were not fully human, any more than the development of some deadly disease in a child makes the child suddenly nonhuman.

The implantation view

An increasingly heard viewpoint today is related to the

implantation of the blastocyst into the uterine lining. This implantation process begins on day six following fertilization and can continue until around day nine. Some now suggest that it is not until this time that the zygote can be called human life. However, achieving implantation does not make the individual more human; rather, implantation makes the individual more likely to survive.

Interestingly enough, the popularity of this view has led to some changes in how some define conception. Until recently, *conception* was synonymous with *fertilization*. In fact, in the 26th edition of *Stedman's Medical Dictionary*, conception was defined as the "act of conceiving, or becoming pregnant; fertilization of the oocyte (ovum) by a spermatozoon to form a viable zygote."[5] Conception was defined as the time of fertilization.

However, something interesting happened in the next five years. In the 27th edition of *Stedman's Medical Dictionary*, conception is defined as follows: "Act of conceiving; the implantation of the blastocyte in the endometrium."[6] Note here that *implantation* is now the defining point in conception. The scientific community arbitrarily, without any scientific justification, redefined the starting point of life.

According to the redefined view, a zygote less than nine or so days old, having not yet completed implantation, would not be considered alive. If it is not alive, it certainly cannot be human. This change was completely arbitrary, for there was no basic change in the understanding of the developmental process that would make this redefinition necessary.

The new definition would, however, have great implications in the political, ethical, and moral arenas. Personal and governmental decision-making on such issues as embryonic stem cell research, cloning, and the so-called "morning after pill" directly depends on the validity of this definition. If preimplantation blastocysts were not really alive, they could be guiltlessly harvested or destroyed prior to the six-to-nine day mark because "conception" had not yet occurred.

The embryological view

The embryological view holds that human life begins 12–14 days after fertilization, the time period after which identical twins would not occur. (*Embryo* can refer to the developing baby at two to three weeks after fertilization or more loosely to all the stages from zygote to fetus.) No individuality and therefore no humanness is considered to exist until it is not possible for twinning to happen. Here, the initial zygote is not human and possesses no aspect of "personhood." As stated previously, this line of reasoning fails because of the shortcoming of the twinning argument itself. Specifically, the fact that conjoined (Siamese) twins are distinct persons is undeniable; their humanity is not obviated by the fact that they share body parts.

The neurologic view

In this view, human life begins when the brain of the fetus has developed enough to generate a recognizable pattern on an electroencephalogram (EEG). Here, it is proposed that humanness is attained when the brain has matured to the point that the appropriate neural pathways have developed.[7] This point is reached at about 26 weeks after fertilization. After this level of maturation has been achieved, the fetus is presumably able to engage in mental activity consistent with being human.

Others take a different view of neurological maturation and propose that human life begins at around 20 weeks gestation. This is the time when the thalamus, a portion of the brain that is centrally located, is formed. The thalamus is involved in processing information before the information reaches the cerebral cortex and also is a part of a complex system of neural connections that play a role in consciousness.

These distinctions are arbitrary. The developing brain does display some electrical activity before the 26-week mark. It could just as easily be argued that any brain activity would constitute humanness.

The ecological view

Proponents of the ecological view hold that the fetus is human when it reaches a level of maturation when it can exist outside the mother's womb.[8] In other words, a fetus is human when it can live separated from its mother. Here the limiting factor is usually not neurological development, but rather the degree of maturation of the lungs.

This view of humanness presents a very interesting problem. The problem is that, over the last century, we have been becoming human earlier and earlier. Here the issue is not the actual stage of development of the fetus. The limiting factor rather is the current state of medical technology. For example, some 20 years ago the age of viability of a prematurely born fetus was about 28 weeks; today it is around 24 weeks. Thus, in this view, man himself, through his advances in technology, can grant humanness where it did not previously exist!

The birthday view

Some hold the position that human life begins only at the point when the baby is born. Here the baby is human when the umbilical cord is cut, and the child survives based on the adequate functioning of its own lungs, circulatory system, etc.

The shortcoming of this reasoning is that even after birth, the child is not truly independent of its mother. Without care from someone, an infant would die very shortly after birth. This supposed "independence" is very much an arbitrary concept.

Other views

There are still other points of view as to the question of when human life begins. Some suggest that a fetus is human when the mother can feel it move in the womb. Others say that humanness begins when the child takes its first breath on its own. Francis Crick, one of the codiscoverers of the structure of DNA, says that a child should not be declared "human" until three days after birth.[9]

There are clearly significant differences in the way that the scientific community views the beginning of life. There is no obvious consensus among scientists about when human life begins. So, can science really help us answer this question? Perhaps science, by its nature, is not capable of dealing directly with this problem. Scott Gilbert, PhD, professor of biology at Swarthmore College, notes, "If one does not believe in a 'soul,' then one need not believe in a moment of ensoulment. The moments of fertilization, gastrulation, neurulation, and birth, are then milestones in the gradual acquisition of what it is to be human. While one may have a particular belief in when the embryo becomes human, it is difficult to justify such a belief solely by science."[10]

If not science, then what?

If science cannot give us the answer, then is there another place we can turn? As Christians, we should turn to the Bible, God's Word, to see if there is a solution to this dilemma.

Psalm 139:13–16

Perhaps the most often quoted portion of Scripture on this subject is Psalm 139:13–16.

> For You formed my inward parts:
> You covered me in my mother's womb.
> I will praise You, for I am fearfully and

wonderfully made;
Marvelous are Your works,
And that my soul knows very well.
My frame was not hidden from You,
When I was made in secret,
And skillfully wrought in the lowest parts of the earth.
Your eyes saw my substance, being yet unformed.
And in Your book they all were written,
The days fashioned for me,
When as yet there were none of them.

Here we read about God knowing the Psalmist while he was "yet unformed," while he was being "made in secret," in a place invisible to human eyes. The uses of the personal pronouns in these verses indicate that there was, indeed, a person present before birth. R.C. Sproul notes, "Scripture does assume a continuity of life from before the time of birth to after the time of birth. The same language and the same personal pronouns are used indiscriminately for both stages."[11]

Jeremiah 1:4–5

Then the word of the Lord came to me, saying:
"Before I formed you in the womb I knew you;
Before you were born I sanctified you;
I ordained you a prophet to the nations."

Here God tells Jeremiah that he was set apart before he was born. This would indicate that there was personhood present before Jeremiah's birth. The verse even indicates that God considered Jeremiah a person and that he was known before he was formed. Sproul indicates, "Even those who do not agree that life begins before birth grant that there is continuity between a child that is conceived and a child that is born. Every child has a past before birth. The issue is this: Was that past personal, or was it impersonal with personhood beginning only at birth?"[12]

Psalm 51:5

This verse is frequently used to make the case for human life beginning at conception. It reads:

> Behold, I was brought forth in iniquity,
> And in sin my mother conceived me.

The most often heard interpretation of this passage is that the author, David, sees that he was sinful even at the time he was conceived. If he was not a person, then it follows that he could not have a sinful human nature at that time. A prehuman mass of cells could not have any basis for morality. Only the "humanness" occurring at the time of conception would allow David to possess a sinful nature at that time.

Life before birth

These Scriptures reveal that there is personhood before birth. The personal nature of the references in the Bible shows how God views the unborn child. Another text frequently used to prove the humanness of the fetus is found in the first chapter of Luke:

> Now Mary arose in those days and went into the hill country with haste, to a city of Judah, and entered the house of Zacharias and greeted Elizabeth. And it happened, when Elizabeth heard the greeting of Mary, that the babe leaped in her womb; and Elizabeth was filled with the Holy Spirit. Then she spoke out with a loud voice and said, "Blessed are you among women, and blessed is the fruit of your womb! But why is this granted to me, that the mother of my Lord should come to me? For indeed, as soon as the voice of your greeting sounded in my ears, the babe leaped in my womb for joy" (Luke 1:39-44).

We read in this passage of a meeting between Mary the mother of Jesus and Elizabeth, her cousin, the mother of John the Baptist. Here Elizabeth describes the life in her womb as "the babe." God's inspired Word reports Elizabeth's assessment that John "leaped" in the womb because of the presence of Jesus. Some try to discount this episode as a miracle, claiming it does not relate to the personhood of the unborn. Nonetheless, God's Word describes this unborn child as capable of exhibiting joy in the presence of his Savior.

Are the unborn of less worth?

Exodus 21 has been put forth by some to suggest the God himself holds that the life of an unborn is less valuable than the life of an adult.

> If men fight, and hurt a woman with child, so that she gives birth prematurely, yet no harm follows, he shall surely be punished accordingly as the woman's husband imposes on him; and he shall pay as the judges determine. But if any harm follows, then you shall give life for life, eye for eye, tooth for tooth, hand for hand, foot for foot . . . (Exodus 21:22–24).

This verse gives directions for dealing with a situation in which two men are fighting and they accidentally harm a pregnant woman. Two circumstances are noted here. The first situation is when the woman gives birth prematurely and "no harm follows." The common interpretation states that here the child is lost due to a premature birth, and the woman herself does not suffer a serious injury. Here the penalty is a fine of some type to compensate for the loss of the child.

The second circumstance is "if any harm follows." Here the common interpretation is that is the woman gives birth prematurely, the child dies, and the woman herself dies. Here the penalty is life for life. It is argued that since there is only a fine imposed in the first circumstance for the loss of only the premature child while the death penalty is imposed for the loss of the mother, the unborn is less valuable than an adult. Thus, the unborn need not be considered to have achieved full humanness before birth.

However, upon closer examination, this type of interpretation may not be valid. The "harm" indicated in these verses may refer to the child and not to the mother. In the first circumstance, the injured mother gives birth prematurely and no "harm" comes to the child. In other words, the premature child lives. Thus, a fine is levied for causing the premature birth and the potential danger involved. In the second situation, there is a premature birth and the "harm" that follows is the death of the child. Here the penalty is life for life. Therefore, the Bible does not hold that the life of the unborn is less valuable than the life of an adult.

John Frame, in the book *Medical Ethics*, says this, "There is *nothing* in Scripture that even remotely suggests that the unborn child is anything less *than a human person from the moment of conception*"[13] (emphasis his). Here, conception is meant to imply the time of fertilization.

So where are we?

A purely scientific examination of human development from the moment of fertilization until birth provides no experimental method that can gauge humanness. Stages of maturation have been described and cataloged. Chemical processes and changes in size and shape have been analyzed. Electrical activity has been monitored. However, even with this vast amount of knowledge, there is no consensus among scientists as to where along this marvelous chain of events an embryo (or zygote or fetus or baby, depending upon who is being asked) becomes human.

Science has, however, revealed the intricate developmental continuum from fertilization, through maturation, to the birth of the child. Each stage flows seamlessly into the next with a myriad of detailed embryological changes followed by organ growth and finely tuned development choreographed with precision. The more we learn about the process, the more amazingly complex we find it to be.

Life begins at conception

Although science has shown us the wonderful continuity of the development of life throughout all its stages, science has been unable to define the onset of humanness. However, there is ample information in Scripture for us to determine the answer to this problem.

The Bible contains numerous references to the unborn.[14] Each time the Bible speaks of the unborn, there is reference to an actual person, a living human being already in existence. These Scriptures, taken in context, all indicate that God considers the unborn to be people. The language of the text continually describes them in personal terms.

Since the Bible treats those persons yet unborn as real persons, and since the development of a person is a continuum with a definite beginning at the moment of fertilization, the logical point at which a person begins to be human is at that beginning. The answer is that life begins at conception (using the now older definition of the term, here to be synonymous with fertilization). Frankly, no other conclusion is possible from Scripture or science.

What are the implications of this conclusion? Why is this important? Quite simply, the status of the zygote/embryo/fetus is central to many issues facing our society. The most obvious issue in this regard is abortion. If the zygote is a human life, then abortion is murder. The same can be said of issues surrounding the embryonic stem cell debate. If the embryo is human, then destroying it is murder, no matter what supposedly altruistic reason is given as justification. The ethics of cloning require consideration of the concept of humanness and the timing of its onset. A person's acceptance or rejection of the controversial morning after pill is based upon the determination of when human life begins.[15]

Complex issues may not have simple solutions, but when examined objectively in light of God's Word, without biases introduced by other motivations, God's truth will reveal the correct answers. Science can give us better understanding of the world God created, and what we see in God's world will agree with the truth we read in God's Word. We dare not play word games with human life to justify personal agendas. Scripture provides no real loopholes or escape clauses to excuse us from the principle that God created human beings in His own image, designed them to reproduce after their kind, and sent Jesus Christ into the world as a human being to die for us all, thus demonstrating the inestimable love our Creator has for each human life.

1. The answer to the question "What is life?" is beyond the scope of this article. There are several excellent resources dealing with this topic: James Stambaugh, "'Life' According to the Bible, and the Scientific Evidence," *TJ* 6, no. 2 (1992): 98–121, online at www.answersingenesis.org/tj/v6/i2/life.asp.

2. This process, called *differentiation*, is the process by which the dividing cells gradually become different from one another.

3. The name of the rapidly diving ball of cells continues to change as size and shape changes, with the name *embryo* being assigned at about three weeks after fertilization. The term *fetus* is used from about the eighth week of development.

4. Christian Answers Net, "Does Life Begin Only When the Embryo Implants?" www.christiananswers.net/q-sum/q-life014.html.

5. *Stedman's Medical Dictionary*, 26th edition (Baltimore: Williams & Wilkins, 1995), p. 377.

6. *Stedman's Medical Dictionary*, 27th edition (Baltimore: Williams & Wilkins, 2000), p. 394.

7. H. J. Morowitz and J. S. Trefil, *The Facts of Life: Science and the Abortion Controversy* (New York: Oxford University Press, 1992).

8. Scott Gilbert, "When Does Human Life Begin?" *Developmental Biology* 8th ed. Online, 8e.devbio.com/article.php?ch=21&id=7.

9. Mark Blocher, *Vital Signs* (Chicago: Moody Press, 1992), p. 91.

10. Gilbert, "When Does Human Life Begin?"

11. R.C. Sproul, *Abortion: A Rational Look at an Emotional Issue* (Colorado Springs: NavPress, 1990), pp. 53–54.

12. Ibid., p. 55.

13. John Frame, *Medical Ethics* (Phillipsburg, NJ: Presbyterian and Reformed Publishing Company, 1988), p. 95.

14. See also Genesis 25:21–23; Isaiah 45.

15. David Menton, "Plan B: Over-the-Counter Abortion?" Answers in Genesis,www.answersin genesis.org/articles/am/v2/n1/plan-b.

Tommy Mitchell graduated with a BA with highest honors from the University of Tennessee–Knoxville in 1980 with a major in cell biology and a minor in biochemistry. He subsequently attended Vanderbilt University School of Medicine in Nashville, where he was granted an MD degree in 1984.

Dr. Mitchell's residency was completed at Vanderbilt University Affiliated Hospitals in 1987. He was board certified in internal medicine, with a medical practice in Gallatin, Tennessee (the city of his birth). In 1991, he was elected to the Fellowship in the American College of Physicians (F.A.C.P.). Tommy became a full-time speaker, researcher, and writer with Answers in Genesis –USA in 2006.

Stem Cells

by Georgia Purdom

Preserving life—it is extremely important in the Christian faith. But what is the biblical definition of life, and how does this definition affect stem cell research?

God clearly commands in Exodus 20:13: "You shall not murder [the intentional, predatory killing of another]" (NIV; see also Matthew 19:18; Romans 13:9). A big controversy today is that of determining when life begins. In the field of embryonic stem cell research (ESCR), this determination is especially crucial. Because technology is advancing faster than society's ethics, we are left to solve such dilemmas in the midst of active research. Determining the ethics in these issues is especially difficult when the research promises to cure diseases that leave millions disabled or dying every year. However, the Bible clearly prohibits evil means to accomplish good ends (Romans 3:8). To develop a biblical worldview of ESCR, we first must sort fact from fiction.

In a recent Pew Research poll, 56% of Americans said it is more important to conduct stem cell research that may lead to new medical cures than to avoid destroying human embryos during the research.[1]

Definitions and the beginning of life

A "stem cell" is an unspecialized cell with the capacity to change into many different cell types, such as blood, muscle, and nerve cells. Two main categories of stem cells are found in embryos and adults. Embryonic stem cells (ESC) are derived from human embryos shortly after fertilization (union of egg and sperm) in a lab dish and are considered to be "totipotent," meaning that they can form any other type of cell in the human body. Adult stem cells are derived from varying locations in adults and are considered to be "pluripotent" or "multipotent" because they can give rise to some but not all the cells in a human body.

Harvesting ESCs kills the embryo, but harvesting adult stem cells does not kill or harm the adult. Many involved with the research of embryonic stem cells do not believe a new person begins at conception or don't care. (See chapter 1 for a discussion of the beginning of life.) Embryonic stem cells are viewed as property, not people. However, the Bible clearly indicates that life does begin at conception (Psalm 51:5, 139:13–15; Jeremiah 1:5). We are made in God's image and are image bearers from conception to death (Genesis 1:27).[2] Therefore, harvesting ESCs violates God's commandment not to murder.

Therapeutic uses of stem cells

Researchers promise many cures as a result of ESCR, and the media tout a world free of Alzheimer's, Parkinson's, multiple sclerosis, spinal cord injuries, and cancer. But, so far these claims have gone unrealized. President Bush's 2001 ban[3] on government-supported research using new ESCs slowed progress in this area, but President Obama lifted the ban in 2009.[4] Less reported in the media is that ESCs have been found to have great genetic instability (mutations and chromosomal changes) that is associated with tumor formation.[5] If these ESCs are used in therapy, they could actually do more harm than good. In addition, anyone receiving these cells will need to take anti-rejection medicine their entire lives since the cells are not a genetic match.

Also underreported is the fact that doctors have currently treated more than 70 different diseases and defects using adult stem cells.[6] Although adult stem cells are more difficult to find and grow in the lab, they are more genetically stable. One type of cell, the Multi-Potent Adult Progenitor Cell (MAPC), has been found that may be able to form many different cell types, such as an ESC.[7] It seems that adult stem cells have great, untapped potential.

Ethical alternatives to embryonic stem cell research

Adult stem cells provide only one of several ethical alternatives to ESCR.[8] They can be harvested from the individual who needs therapy without worry of cell rejection.

A recent article in *Nature*[9] indicates it may be possible to reprogram an adult cell to become more like an ESC. Currently this technology depends on the use of an ESC to reprogram the adult cell, but it is hoped that this requirement can be overcome.

Several ethical alternatives to embryonic stem cell research that hold great promise are available.

Another popular alternative is to use umbilical cord blood. Since umbilical cord blood is rich in stem cells, it is collected shortly after birth. These blood cells have been used to successfully treat many diseases in adults and children.[10] Several companies store such blood for a fee.[11] The stem cells can then be used if needed later in life by that individual or possibly by their family.

Stem cells found in baby teeth[12] are capable of becoming several different types of cells, including neural cells. Such cells are extracted from the pulp of a tooth that a child has lost as a result of the transition to permanent teeth. Dr. Songtao Shi, discoverer of these cells, says this about their future, "We can ask parents to put [baby] teeth that comes out in milk, put it in the refrigerator and give a call the next day, and we can get stem cells out. You can freeze them in nitrogen and save them for years and years."[13] These cells hold great promise for use in future therapies.

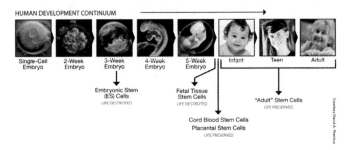

HUMAN DEVELOPMENT CONTINUUM

Single-Cell Embryo   2-Week Embryo   3-Week Embryo   4-Week Embryo   5-Week Embryo   Infant   Teen   Adult

Embryonic Stem (ES) Cells
LIFE DESTROYED

Fetal Tissue Stem Cells
LIFE DESTROYED

"Adult" Stem Cells
LIFE PRESERVED

Cord Blood Stem Cells
Placental Stem Cells
LIFE PRESERVED

Courtesy David A. Prentice

The process cannot be justified

Although ESCR is highly publicized as a possible means to put an end to many debilitating diseases, the murder of a human being is not justified. Many less popularized means, such as the ones previously mentioned, have already begun treating and bringing an end to these same diseases, and without the need to destroy human life.

Although everyone wants to see such devastating diseases come to an end, we all must realize our work will only lead to a temporary alleviation. Jesus Christ, the true conqueror of disease and death, will create a new heaven and a new earth where the effects of sin have been removed. That is the cure we eagerly await.

---

1.   The Pew Research Center, "Most Want Middle Ground on Abortion," http://pewforum.org/publications/surveys/social-issues-06.pdf.

2.   For a fuller discussion of euthanasia go to http://www.equip.org/DE197-1.

3.   See http://www.whitehouse.gov/news/releases/2001/08/20010809-2.html.

4.   See http://www.whitehouse.gov/the_press_office/Removing-Barriers-to-Responsible-Scientific-Research-Involving-Human-Stem-Cells/

5.   Anirban Maitra et al., "Genomic Alterations in Cultured Human Embryonic Stem Cells," *Nature Genetics* 37 (2005): 1099–1103.

6.   See www.stemcellresearch.org/facts/treatments.htm.

7.   Sylvia Westphal, "Ultimate Stem Cell Discovered," *NewScientist*, http://www.newscientist.com/article/dn1826.

8.   In August 2006, scientists claimed to have harvested ESCs without killing the embryo, but this was later shown not to be the case.

9.   J. Silva et al., "Nanog Promotes Transfer of Pluripotency after Cell Fusion," *Nature* 441 (2006): 997–1001.

---

10. Mary Laughlin et al., "Outcomes after Transplantation of Cord Blood or Bone Marrow from Unrelated Donors in Adults with Leukemia," *New England Journal of Medicine* 351 no. 22 (2004): 2265–2275.

11. National Marrow Donor Program, http://www.marrow.org/ABOUT/About_Us/index.html.

12. Masako Miura et al., "SHED: Stem Cells from Human Exfoliated Deciduous Teeth," *Proceedings of the National Academy of Sciences* 100 no. 10 (2003): 5807–5812.

13. Steven Ertelt, "Baby Teeth Offer Another Effesctive Source of Adult Stem Cells," http://www.christianliferesources.com/?news/view.php&newsid=3788.

 **Georgia Purdom** earned her doctorate in molecular genetics from Ohio State University. She spent six years as a professor of biology at Mt. Vernon Nazarene University before joining the staff at Answers in Genesis–USA. Dr. Purdom is also a member of the American Society for Microbiology and American Society for Cell Biology.

Planned Parenthood: Its History and Philosophy

by Wendy Wright

Not many organizations achieve the impact that Planned Parenthood (PP) has had on Western culture. At its root is an evolutionary philosophy taken to its logical conclusion that man is merely an animal in the process of evolving to his ultimate potential. Largely at public expense, PP promotes the taking of human life while denigrating biblical morality and the sanctity of human life.

In 2005 alone, Planned Parenthood received an incredible $882 million in gross revenue, with $63 million in "excess revenue" (profit). About a third of this gross revenue comes from U.S. taxpayers, and another hefty chunk comes from American corporations and foundations.[1] This international "nonprofit" organization has over 120 affiliates operating more than 850 local health centers across the U.S., plus 78 partner organizations in 29 countries.

Photo courtesy Library of Congress

Margaret Sanger established the American Birth Control League (now known as Planned Parenthood). She also launched a newspaper advocating birth control called *The Woman Rebel*, which was declared vulgar and pornographic at the time. After being indicted for violation of postal laws for this new publication, Sanger fled to England to escape prosecution but returned later to continue the fight for her cause.

PP began as the dream of Margaret Sanger, a pro-eugenic, pro-abortion advocate.[1] Between 1920 and 1922, Sanger launched the American Birth Control League (ABCL), the forerunner of Planned Parenthood. This organization was founded to maintain a so-called "fit" nation and keep society from being filled with, in the words of Sanger, "the most far-reaching peril to the future of civilization" (referring to people of different ethnic groups).[1] The ABCL thus targeted low-income families as those most in need of birth control.

In 1942 after the Nazi horrors discredited outright eugenics (killing the "unfit" in order to breed a "master race"), the ABCL was renamed Planned Parenthood. At that time the organization's affiliates made legal access to unrestricted abortion a high priority. As one medical director stated, "You can't get adequate fertility control with contraception alone. You have got to grapple with sterilization and abortion."[1]

Therefore, PP began pressuring governments to limit births through incentives and punishments. It also called China's brutal one-child campaign a "stunning success."[1] Government entitlement programs currently pay for much of PP's lucrative business based, in part, on the idea that it will reduce welfare costs by reducing the number of people.

The organization claims to be a leading protector of a woman's right to choose, a provider of contraceptives, a champion in the battle against sexually transmitted diseases (STDs), and a proponent of public education on the subject. But these claims really just divert attention from the foundational goal of limiting the procreation of society's "unfit."[2] PP's promotion of immorality without consequences—which is being taught in educational programs worldwide—actually leads to an increase in STDs, not a decrease. The Bible-based principle of abstinence until marriage and fidelity within marriage is ignored.

Planned Parenthood promotes "values-free" education that denigrates morality and parental authority.

The organization also seeks to ensure that pro-life laws are overturned while it insists that the 1973 U.S. Supreme Court decision that legalized abortion (*Roe v. Wade*—see section below for more details) must not be reversed. It also mocks Bible-believing Christians while hiring liberal clergy and establishing alliances with liberal churches.[2]

Creative and courageous people are countering Planned Parenthood through pro-life pregnancy care centers, legislation, and programs that promote abstinence until marriage and fidelity in marriage. Also, tens of thousands of churches and millions of Christians annually honor Sanctity of Life Sunday.

Even so, one of our most powerful tactics to support life is one that Planned Parenthood defies: "Be fruitful and multiply" (Genesis 1:28) and then to train up the next generation in the "training and admonition of the Lord" (Ephesians 6:4), which would include upholding the authority of the Bible and the sanctity of life.

Wendy Wright is president of Concerned Women for America, the nation's largest public-policy women's organization. Wendy helps promote legislation and international policies that are beneficial to women and families, and she briefs congressional and administration staff on pro-family issues.

For more information on Planned Parenthood, see CWA's paper: "The Negro Project: Margaret Sanger's Eugenic Plan for Black Americans" (available at www.cwfa.org).

The Facts of Roe v. Wade

The aftershock of 1973's landmark Supreme Court decision *Roe v. Wade*, which legalized abortion in all 50 U.S. states, continues to divide people into pro-abortion and pro-life camps. Its impact is well-known, but its history is not.

The case, which tested a Texas law that criminalized abortion unless the mother's life was at risk, began in March 1970 when 21-year-old Norma L. McCorvey ("Jane Roe") filed suit against Dallas County District Attorney Henry Wade. McCorvey wanted an abortion but was prohibited by state law. She took her case to court, and the three-judge district court ruled in her favor. The case was then appealed and taken to the highest court in the country—the U.S. Supreme Court. On January 22, 1973, the Supreme Court ruled that the Texas law violated women's Fourteenth Amendment right to privacy.

Since 1973, legal challenges have limited the reach of the case but have not overturned it. Every year on the anniversary of this decision, protesters demonstrate outside the Supreme Court building in Washington, D.C. Tens of thousands of churches across the United States observe the anniversary as National Sanctity of Human Life Day, which President George W. Bush declared to be "an opportunity to strengthen our resolve in creating a society where every life has meaning and our most vulnerable members are protected and defended including unborn children, the sick and dying, and persons with disabilities and birth defects."

---

1. George Grant, *Killer Angel: A Short Biography of Planned Parenthood's Founder, Margaret Sanger* (Nashville: Highland Books, 2001).

2. George Grant, *Grand Illusions: The Legacy of Planned Parenthood* (Brentwood, TN: Wolgemuth and Hyatt, 1989).

Wendy Wright is president of Concerned Women for America, the nation's largest public-policy women's organization. Wendy helps promote legislation and international policies that are beneficial to women and families, and she briefs congressional and administration staff on pro-family issues.

Cloning: Right or Wrong?

by Werner Gitt

A recent book, *In the Beginning, There was Dolly*, says:

> The lamb has always been a symbol of innocence. This changed abruptly in the spring of 1997. "Dolly," a barely three-month-old sheep, hit the headlines, displacing politicians and pop stars from the front pages of newspapers and magazines. Overnight, the fluffy white "lamb of innocence" had become a symbol of threat to human society through an eerie new technology—cloning.[1]

Why all the fuss? Because Dolly was a genetically identical copy of an adult sheep—a clone. She was the first such clone of a mammal.

How Dolly was born

In 1996, Ian Wilmut succeeded in awakening the hidden information of the nucleus of such a cell from its slumber. Wilmut's experiment involved three adult female sheep. He first took an udder cell from sheep A, a six-year-old of the Finn-Dorset breed. He then fused the genetic information in its nucleus with an egg cell from sheep B, from which the nucleus had been removed. Tiny electric shocks were used to stimulate this new "combination" egg cell to divide. Finally, the resultant embryo was implanted into the womb of sheep C, where it developed just like any other sheep embryo.

150 days later, Dolly became the first sheep to be born without a father. Mice have now also been cloned from an adult. This

was using a cumulus cell, a type which surrounds the ovary, and a slightly different technique. These clones have also been cloned—and these again—three generations of healthy clones. Cattle, and many other animals, have since been cloned as well.

Dolly was the first genetically identical copy of an *adult*. As a fertilized egg cell progressively splits, its millions of offspring cells specialize into muscle cells, skin cells or secretory cells, for example.

It was thought that a specialized cell could never revert to become a non-differentiated cell, with all the genetic instructions to form the entire creature "unmasked." However, we now know that even adult mammals can be cloned.

Examining cloning

But how do we judge cloning according to the Bible? In answering, we will first give some biological background.

The cells of a living being—whether in the skin, lungs, nose or elsewhere—have a complete set of genetic "instructions," known as the genome. From the very first division of the fertilized egg, the nucleus of each cell formed by successive cell divisions stores the *complete* genetic information.

At a very early stage of embryonic development, the cells specialize (or differentiate) so that some become nerve cells, some skin cells etc. Each performs different functions, based on different parts of the genetic code. That part of the genome which is not needed for the specialized function of a gland cell, for example, is not lost but is switched off or "asleep."

Dolly is a copy, a clone of the sheep whose udder cell was used. A clone (from Greek *klon*) is an individual—plant, animal or human being—derived by asexual reproduction from another organism that has the identical hereditary components. Individuals could derive from the same cell (identical twins), or the clone could originate from the cell of another individual.

But, in spite of the fact that clones have the same genotype, they are never absolutely identical. The way an individual develops depends to a high degree on the surroundings, too.

Cloning is not a human invention. The Creator Himself planned this way of reproduction. When we plant potato tubers of the previous year, the potatoes we later harvest are just as nutritious and tasty. This is because there was no new combination of hereditary information, with one plant being pollinated with the DNA of another. They are in fact clones of the previous year's plant.

Strawberries are also propagated from runners which are actually clones of the parent plant, bearing fruit with the same color and taste.

We also see cloning in the animal kingdom. Aphids can reproduce both sexually and by cloning. In spring the first aphid generation hatches out of fertilized eggs. Later, the aphid lays eggs that start to divide without being fertilized—they are clones of the mother. Many other animals reproduce by cloning: certain bees, ants, crustaceans, and lizards.

Concerning people, we know that identical twins are real clones. The fertilized egg splits in two, and each of these two "daughter" cells develops separately. They are individual people with an absolutely identical set of genes. Because of this they have the same innate gifts and talents, as well as the same predisposition to particular illnesses. They have the same color hair and eyes, the same shoe size and the same features. But, in spite of this, they are two different people: each of them experiences the world in a unique way, and each is uniquely molded by his or her individual experiences and choices. Both have their own personality, and their own soul.

A biblical view

So is humanity allowed to use the cloning technique? Humans are appointed rulers over "the fish of the sea, over the birds of the air, and over every living thing that moves on the earth" (Genesis 1:28). So I see no reason why it should not be used *in plants and animals*. Especially where there is a benefit to mankind, such as less hunger or disease. Christ's example indicates that things (such as healing, binding wounds, peace-making, and feeding the hungry) which oppose the effects of the Curse are "blessed."

When humans breed wheat that can be cultivated in cold areas, or use artificial selection to get cows yielding more milk, we are also "manipulating nature." But of course, few would (or should) oppose such intervention. I think that God's instruction to humans to subdue the earth (Genesis 1:28) also allows for cloning.

The world-wide fear of cloning derives from a vague and confused anxiety about a technology that seems out of control. Günther Stockinger wrote in the German news magazine *Der Spiegel*, chronicling the year 1997:

> Biologists and doctors anywhere in the world could hit upon the idea of generating genetically identical copies of geniuses, top-class athletes, artists or movie stars. The person off the shelf, or "*Homo xerox*", would no longer be mere fiction. Even Hitlers and Stalins could be produced in the labs of bio-modelers if only one usable cell of theirs could be found.

A major reason for this fear is that in today's "evolutionized" world, there is no dividing line between the animal kingdom and humans, so the same ethical standards apply to dealings with both.

The Bible, however, draws a clear line between animals and humans, and gives us ethical guidelines:

- Humans were created separately, in God's image, unlike the animal kingdom (Genesis 1:27). Our existence extends beyond physical death (Luke 16:19–31, Philippians 1:23). This is nowhere indicated for animals.

- God allowed humans to kill animals (Genesis 9:2–3). Concerning other humans, He gave the commandment: "You shall not murder [the Hebrew ratsach means murder, not simply kill]" (Exodus 20:13).

- God entrusted humans with dominion over the animal kingdom (Genesis 1:26). But humans were never told to have dominion over other humans, nor manipulate them, as would be the case if cloning humans.

Furthermore, humans are meant to have fathers and mothers, to be where possible the offspring of a sacred marriage relationship, the family ordained by God. While unfortunate circumstances in a fallen world mean that sometimes children have to be raised by only one parent, a clone could *never* have two parents. *Thus the artificial cloning of a complete human being, because it deliberately sets out to cause such a situation, is opposed to biblical principles.*

There are further reasons for rejecting the artificial cloning of humans. Each fertilized egg, including those from cloning, is a new human individual. Yet perfecting the cloning technique requires many experiments. Many individuals would be enabled to commence life, only to be deliberately destroyed. The research director of a biotechnology firm recently said,

> My own view is that the research [on human cloning] is immoral at the present time and should always be immoral. To make the technique more efficient would require a great deal of experimentation. And to get this more refined would be at the expense of having deformed babies, etc. To get it into a situation where you could clone humans efficiently would have such a history of misery associated with it.[2]

Thus, while it may be right under certain circumstances to clone animals to benefit people, I think it is absolutely wrong to try to clone humans.

---

1. Ingeborg and Josef Cernaj, *Am Anfang war Dolly* (Munich: Wilhelm Heyne Verlag, 1997), p. 207.

2. Dr Alan Colman, of PPL Therapeutics in Edinburgh, quoted in a 1998 Reuters (New York) news release.

Werner Gitt, now retired, was a director and professor at the German Federal Institute of Physics and Technology (Physikalisch-Technische Bundesanstalt, Braunschweig), the Head of the Department of Information Technology.

In addition to the numerous scientific papers in the fields of information science, mathematics, and control engineering, Dr. Gitt has also authored several creationist books including *Did God Use Evolution?*, *If Animals Could Talk*, *In the Beginning was Information*, and *Stars and their Purpose*.

Are There Really Different Races?

by Ken Ham

What if a Chinese person were to marry a Polynesian, or an African with black skin were to marry a Japanese, or a person from India were to marry a person from America with white skin—would these marriages be in accord with biblical principles?

A significant number of Christians would claim that such "interracial" marriages directly violate God's principles in the Bible and should not be allowed.

Does the Word of God really condemn the marriages mentioned above? Is there ultimately any such thing as interracial marriage?

To answer these questions, we must first understand what the Bible and science teach about "race."

What constitutes a "race"?

In the 1800s, before Darwinian evolution was popularized, most people, when talking about "races," would be referring to such groups as the "English race," "Irish race," and so on. However, this all changed in 1859 when Charles Darwin published his book *On the Origin of Species by Means of Natural Selection or the Preservation of Favoured Races in the Struggle for Life.*

Darwinian evolution was (and still is[1]) inherently a racist philosophy, teaching that different groups or "races" of people evolved at different times and rates, so some groups are more like their apelike ancestors than others. Leading evolutionist Stephen Jay

AUSTRALOID

NEGROID

MONGOLOID

EVOLUTIONARY
ANCESTOR

CAUCASOID

RACES

Gould claimed, "Biological arguments for racism may have been common before 1859, but they increased by orders of magnitude following the acceptance of evolutionary theory."[2]

The Australian Aborigines, for instance, were considered the missing links between the apelike ancestor and the rest of mankind.[3] This resulted in terrible prejudices and injustices towards the Australian Aborigines.[4]

Ernst Haeckel, famous for popularizing the now-discredited idea that "ontogeny recapitulates phylogeny," [5] stated:

> At the lowest stage of human mental development are the Australians, some tribes of the Polynesians, and the Bushmen, Hottentots, and some of the Negro tribes. Nothing, however, is perhaps more remarkable in this respect, than that some of the wildest tribes in southern Asia and eastern Africa have no trace whatever of the first foundations of all human civilization, of family life, and marriage. They live together in herds, like apes.[6]

Racist attitudes fueled by evolutionary thinking were largely responsible for an African pygmy being displayed, along with an orangutan, in a cage in the Bronx zoo.[7] Indeed, Congo pygmies were once thought to be "small apelike, elfish creatures" that "exhibit many ape-like features in their bodies."[8]

As a result of Darwinian evolution, many people started thinking in terms of the different people groups around the world representing different "races," but within the context of evolutionary philosophy. This has resulted in many people today, consciously or unconsciously, having ingrained prejudices against certain other groups of people.[9]

However, *all* human beings in the world today are classified as *Homo sapiens sapiens*. Scientists today admit that, biologically, there really is only one race of humans. For instance, a scientist at the Advancement of Science Convention in Atlanta stated, "Race is a social construct derived mainly from perceptions conditioned by events of recorded history, and it has no basic biological reality." This person went on to say, "Curiously enough, the idea comes very close to being of American manufacture."[10]

Reporting on research conducted on the concept of race, ABC News stated, "More and more scientists find that the differences that set us apart are cultural, not racial. Some even say that the word *race* should be abandoned because it's meaningless." The article went on to say that "we accept the idea of race because it's a convenient way of putting people into broad categories, frequently to suppress them—the most hideous example was provided by

GET RID OF THIS *EVOLUTIONIZED* TERM!

Hitler's Germany. And racial prejudice remains common throughout the world."[11]

In an article in the *Journal of Counseling and Development*,[12] researchers argued that the term "race" is basically so meaningless that it should be discarded.

More recently, those working on mapping the human genome announced "that they had put together a draft of the entire sequence of the human genome, and the researchers had unanimously declared, there is only one race—the human race."[13]

Personally, because of the influences of Darwinian evolution and the resulting prejudices, I believe everyone (and especially Christians) should abandon the term "race(s)." We could refer instead to the different "people groups" around the world.

The Bible and "race"

The Bible does not even use the word *race* in reference to people,[14] but it does describe all human beings as being of "one blood" (Acts 17:26). This of course emphasizes that we are all related, as all humans are descendants of the first man, Adam (1 Corinthians 15:45),[15] who was created in the image of God (Genesis 1:26–27).[16] The Last Adam, Jesus Christ (1 Corinthians 15:45) also became a descendant of Adam. Any descendant of Adam can be saved because our mutual relative by blood, Jesus Christ, died and rose again. This is why the gospel can (and should) be preached to all tribes and nations.

Can the Bible be used to justify racist attitudes?

The inevitable question arises, "If the Bible teaches all humans are the same, where was the church during the eras of slavery and segregation? Doesn't the Bible actually condone the enslavement of a human being by another?"

Both the Old and New Testaments of the Bible mention slaves

and slavery. As with all other biblical passages, these must be understood in their grammatical-historical context.

Dr. Walter Kaiser, former president of Gordon-Conwell Theological Seminary and Old Testament scholar, states:

> The laws concerning slavery in the Old Testament appear to function to moderate a practice that worked as a means of loaning money for Jewish people to one another or for handling the problem of the prisoners of war. Nowhere was the institution of slavery as such condemned; but then, neither did it have anything like the connotations it grew to have during the days of those who traded human life as if it were a mere commodity for sale. . . . In all cases the institution was closely watched and divine judgment was declared by the prophets and others for all abuses they spotted.[17]

Job recognized that all were equal before God, and all should be treated as image-bearers of the Creator.

> If I have despised the cause of my male or female servant when they complained against me, what then shall I do when God rises up? When He punishes, how shall I answer Him? Did not He who made me in the womb make them? Did not the same One fashion us in the womb? (Job 31:13–15).

In commenting on Paul's remarks to the slaves in his epistles, Peter H. Davids writes:

> The church never adopted a rule that converts had to give up their slaves. Christians were not under law but under grace. Yet we read in the literature of the second century and later of many masters who upon their conversion freed their slaves. The reality stands that it is difficult to call a person a slave during the week and treat them like a brother or sister in the church. Sooner or later the implications

of the kingdom they experienced in church seeped into the behavior of the masters during the week. Paul did in the end create a revolution, not one from without, but one from within, in which a changed heart produced changed behavior and through that in the end brought about social change. This change happened wherever the kingdom of God was expressed through the church, so the world could see that faith in Christ really was a transformation of the whole person.[18]

Those consistently living out their Christian faith realize that the forced enslavement of another human being goes against the biblical teaching that all humans were created in the image of God and are of equal standing before Him (Galatians 3:28; Colossians 3:11). Indeed, the most ardent abolitionists during the past centuries were Bible-believing Christians. John Wesley, Granville Sharp, William Wilberforce, Jonathan Edwards, Jr., and Thomas Clarkson all preached against the evils of slavery and worked to bring about the abolition of the slave trade in England and North America. Harriet Beecher Stowe conveyed this message in her famous novel *Uncle Tom's Cabin*. And of course, who can forget the change in the most famous of slave traders? John Newton, writer of "Amazing Grace," eventually became an abolitionist after his conversion to Christianity, when he embraced the truth of Scripture.

"Racial" differences

But some people think there must be different races of people because there appear to be major differences between various groups, such as skin color and eye shape.

The truth, though, is that these so-called "racial characteristics" are only minor variations among people groups. If one were to take any two people anywhere in the world, scientists have found that the basic genetic differences between these two people

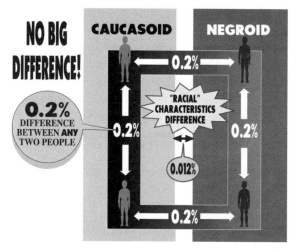

would typically be around 0.2 percent—even if they came from the same people group.[19] But these so-called "racial" characteristics that people think are major differences (skin color, eye shape, etc.) "account for only 0.012 percent of human biological variation."[20]

Dr. Harold Page Freeman, chief executive, president, and director of surgery at North General Hospital in Manhattan, reiterates, "If you ask what percentage of your genes is reflected in your external appearance, the basis by which we talk about race, the answer seems to be in the range of 0.01 percent."[21]

In other words, the so-called "racial" differences are absolutely trivial— overall, there is more variation *within* any group than there is *between* one group and another. If a white person is looking for a tissue match for an organ transplant, for instance, the best match may come from a black person, and vice versa. ABC News claims, "What the facts show is that there are differences among us, but they stem from culture, not race."[22]

The only reason many people think these differences are major is because they've been brought up in a culture that has taught them to see the differences this way. Dr. Douglas C. Wallace, professor of molecular genetics at Emory University School of Medicine in Atlanta, stated, "The criteria that people use for race are based entirely on external features that we are programmed to recognize."[23]

If the Bible teaches and science confirms that all are of the same human race and all are related as descendants of Adam, then why are there such seemingly great differences between us (for example, in skin color)? The answer, again, comes with a biblically informed understanding of science.

Skin "color"

Jesus loves the little children, all the children of the world. Red and yellow, black and white, they are precious in His sight.

When Jesus said, "Let the little children come to Me, and do not forbid them; for of such is the kingdom of heaven" (Matthew 19:14), He did not distinguish between skin colors. In fact, scientists have discovered that there is one major pigment, called melanin, that produces our skin color. There are two main forms of melanin: eumelanin (brown to black) and pheomelanin (red to yellow). These combine to give us the particular shade of skin that we have.[24]

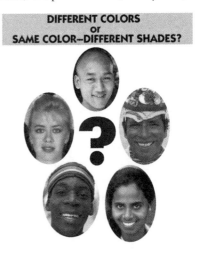

DIFFERENT COLORS or SAME COLOR–DIFFERENT SHADES?

Melanin is produced by melanocytes, which are cells in the bottom layer of the epidermis. No matter what our shade of skin, we all have approximately the same concentration of melanocytes in our bodies. Melanocytes insert melanin into melanosomes, which transfer the melanin into other skin cells, which are cabable of dividing (stem cells), primarily in the lowest layer of the epidermis. According to one expert,

> The melanosomes (tiny melanin-packaging units) are slightly larger and more numerous per cell in dark-skinned than light skinned people. They also do not degrade as readily, and disperse into adjacent skin cells to a higher degree.[25]

In the stem cells, the pigment serves its function as it forms a little dark umbrella over each nucleus. The melanin protects the epidermal cells from being damaged by sunlight. In people with lighter shades of skin, much of the pigment is lost after these cells divide and their daughter cells move up in the epidermis to form the surface dead layer—the stratum corneum.

Geneticists have found that four to six genes, each with multiple alleles (or variations), control the amount and type of melanin produced. Because of this, a wide variety of skin shades exist. In fact, it is quite easy for one couple to produce a wide range of skin shades in just one generation, as will be shown below.

Inheritance

DNA (deoxyribonucleic acid) is the molecule of heredity that is passed from parents to child. In humans, the child inherits 23 chromosomes from each parent (the father donates 23 through his sperm, while the mother donates 23 through her egg). At the moment of conception, these chromosomes unite to form a unique combination of DNA and control much of what makes the child an individual. Each chromosome pair contains hundreds of genes, which regulate the physical development of the child. Note that no new genetic information is generated at conception, but a new *combination* of already-existing genetic information is formed.

To illustrate the basic genetic principles involved in determining skin shade, we'll use a simplified explanation,[26] with just two genes controlling the production of melanin. Let's say that the *A* and *B* versions of the genes code for a lot of melanin, while the *a* and *b* versions code for a small amount of melanin.

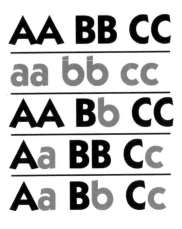

If the father's sperm carried the AB version and the mother's ovum carried the AB, the child would be AABB, with a lot of melanin, and thus very dark skin. Should both parents carry the ab version, the child would be aabb, with very little melanin, and thus very light skin. If the father carries AB (very dark skin) and the mother carries ab (very light skin), the child will be AaBb, with a middle brown shade of skin. In fact, the majority of the world's population has a middle brown skin shade.

A simple exercise with a Punnet Square shows that if each parent has a middle brown shade of skin (AaBb), the combinations that they could produce result in a wide variety of skin shades in just one generation. Based on the skin colors seen today, we can infer that Adam and Eve most likely would have had a middle brown skin color. Their children, and children's children, could have ranged from very light to very dark.

No one really has red, or yellow, or black skin. We all have the same basic color, just different shades of it. We all share the same pigments—our bodies just have different combinations of them.[27]

Melanin also determines eye color. If the iris of the eye has a larger amount of melanin, it will be brown. If the iris has a little melanin, the eye will be blue. (The blue color in blue eyes results from the way light scatters off of the thin layer of brown-colored melanin.)

Hair color is also influenced by the production of melanin. Brown to black hair results from a greater production of melanin, while lighter hair results from less melanin. Those with red hair have a mutation in one gene that causes a greater proportion of the reddish form of melanin (pheomelanin) to be produced.[28]

DNA also controls the basic shape of our eyes. Individuals whose DNA codes for an extra layer of adipose tissue around the eyes have almond-shaped eyes (this is common among Asian people groups). All people groups have adipose tissue around the eyes, some simply have more or less.

Origin of people groups

Those with darker skin tend to live in warmer climates, while those with lighter skin tend to live in colder climates. Why are certain characteristics more prominent in some areas of the world?

We know that Adam and Eve were the first two people. Their descendants filled the earth. However, the world's population was reduced to eight during the Flood of Noah. From these eight individuals have come all the tribes and nations. It is likely that the skin shade of Noah and his family was middle brown. This would enable his sons and their wives to produce a variety of skin shades in just one generation. Because there was a common language and everybody lived in the same general vicinity, barriers that may have prevented their descendants from freely intermarrying weren't as great as they are today. Thus, distinct differences in features and skin color in the population weren't as prevalent as they are today.

In Genesis 11 we read of the rebellion at the Tower of Babel. God judged this rebellion by giving each family group a different language. This made it impossible for the groups to understand each other, and so they split apart, each extended family going its own way, and finding a different place to live. The result was that the people were scattered over the earth.[29]

Because of the new language and geographic barriers, the groups no longer freely mixed with other groups, and the result was a splitting of the gene pool. Different cultures formed, with certain features becoming predominant within each group. The characteristics of each became more and more prominent as new generations of children were born. If we were to travel back in time to Babel, and mix up the people into completely different family groups, then people groups with completely different characteristics might result. For instance, we might find a fair-skinned group with tight, curly dark hair that has blue, almond-shaped eyes. Or a group with very dark skin, blue eyes, and straight brown hair.[30]

Some of these (skin color, eye shape, and so on) became general characteristics of each particular people group through various selection pressures (environmental, sexual, etc.) and/or mutation.[31] For example, because of the protective factor of melanin, those with darker skin would have been more likely to survive in areas where sunlight is more intense (warmer, tropical areas near the equator), as they are less likely to suffer from diseases such as skin cancer. Those with lighter skin lack the melanin needed to protect them from the harmful UV rays, and so may have been more likely to die before they were able to reproduce. UVA radiation also destroys the B vitamin folate, which is necessary for DNA synthesis in cell division. Low levels of folate in pregnant women can lead to defects in the developing baby. Again, because of this, lighter-skinned individuals may be selected against in areas of intense sunlight.

On the flip side, melanin works as a natural sunblock, limiting the sunlight's ability to stimulate the liver to produce vitamin D, which helps the body absorb calcium and build strong bones. Since those with darker skin need more sunlight to produce vitamin D, they may not have been as able to survive as well in areas of less sunlight (northern, colder regions) as their lighter-skinned family members, who don't need as much sunlight to produce adequate amounts of vitamin D. Those lacking vitamin D are more likely to develop diseases such as rickets (which is associated with a calcium deficiency), which can cause slowed growth and bone fractures. It is known that when those with darker skin lived in England during the Industrial Revolution, they were quick to develop rickets because of the general lack of sunlight.[32]

Of course, these are generalities. Exceptions occur, such as in the case of the darker-skinned Inuit tribes living in cold northern regions. However, their diet consists of fish, the oil of which is a ready source of vitamin D, which could account for their survival in this area.

Real science in the present fits with the biblical view that all people are rather closely related—there is only one race biologically. Therefore, to return to our original question, there is, in essence, no such thing as interracial marriage. So we are left with this—is there anything in the Bible that speaks clearly against men and women from different people groups marrying?

The dispersion at Babel

Note that the context of Genesis 11 makes it clear that the reason for God's scattering the people over the earth was that they had united in rebellion against Him. Some Christians point to this event in an attempt to provide a basis for their arguments against so-called interracial marriage. They believe that this passage implies that God is declaring that people from different people groups can't marry so that the nations are kept apart. However, there is no such indication in this passage that what is called "interracial marriage" is condemned. Besides, there has been so much mixing of people groups over the years, that it would be impossible for every human being today to trace their lineage back to know for certain which group(s) they are descended from.

We need to understand that the sovereign creator God is in charge of the nations of this world. Paul makes this very clear in Acts 17:26. Some people erroneously claim this verse to mean that people from different nations shouldn't marry. However, this passage has nothing to do with marriage. As John Gill makes clear in his classic commentary, the context is that God is in charge of all things—where, how, and for how long any person, tribe, or nation will live, prosper, and perish.[33]

In all of this, God is working to redeem for Himself a people who are one in Christ. The Bible makes clear in Galatians 3:28, Colossians 3:11, and Romans 10:12–13 that in regard to salvation, there is no distinction between male or female or Jew or Greek. In Christ, any separation between people is broken down. As Christians, we are one in Christ and thus have a common purpose—to live for Him who made us. This oneness in Christ is vitally important to understanding marriage.

Purpose of marriage

Malachi 2:15 informs us that an important purpose of marriage is to produce godly offspring—progeny that are trained in the ways of the Lord. Jesus (in Matthew 19) and Paul (in Ephesians 5) make it clear that when a man and woman marry, they become one flesh (because they were one flesh historically—Eve was made from Adam). Also, the man and woman must be one spiritually so they can fulfill the command to produce godly offspring.

This is why Paul states in 2 Corinthians 6:14, "Do not be unequally yoked together with unbelievers. For what fellowship has righteousness with lawlessness? And what communion has light with darkness?"

According to the Bible then, which of the following marriages in the picture on the right does God counsel against entering into?

The answer is obvious—number 3. According to the Bible, the priority in marriage is that a Christian should marry only a Christian.

Sadly, there are some Christian homes where the parents are more concerned about their children not marrying someone from another "race" than whether or

not they are marrying a Christian. When Christians marry non-Christians, it negates the spiritual (not the physical) oneness in marriage, resulting in negative consequences for the couple and their children.[34]

Roles in marriage

Of course, every couple needs to understand and embrace the biblical roles prescribed for each family member.[35] Throughout the Scriptures our special roles and responsibilities are revealed. Consider these piercing passages directed to fathers:

> The father shall make known Your truth to the children (Isaiah 38:19).

> Fathers, do not provoke your children to wrath, but bring them up in the training and admonition of the Lord (Ephesians 6:4).

> For I have known him, in order that he may command his children and his household after him, that they keep the way of the Lord, to do righteousness and justice, that

the Lord may bring to Abraham what He has spoken to him (Genesis 18:19).

These are just a few of the many verses that mention fathers in regard to training children. Additionally, the writer of Psalm 78 continually admonishes fathers to teach their children so they'll not forget to teach their children, so that they might not forget what God has done and keep His commandments. This includes building within their children a proper biblical world-view and providing them with answers to the questions the world asks about God and the Bible (as this book does). It also includes shepherding and loving his wife as Christ loved the church (Ephesians 5:25–27).

Of course, just as God made the role of the man clear, He has also made His intentions known regarding the role of a godly wife. In the beginning, God fashioned a woman to complete what was lacking in Adam, that she might become his helper, that the two of them would truly become one (Genesis 2:15–25). In other Bible passages the woman is encouraged to be a woman of character, integrity, and action (e.g., Proverbs 31:10–31). Certainly mothers should also be involved in teaching their children spiritual truths.

These roles are true for couples in every tribe and nation.

Rahab and Ruth

The examples of Rahab and Ruth help us understand how God views the issue of marriage between those who are from different people groups but trust in the true God.

Rahab was a Canaanite. These Canaanites had an ungodly culture and were descendants of Canaan, the son of Ham. Remember, Canaan was cursed because of his obvious rebellious nature. Sadly, many people state that Ham was cursed—but this is not true.[36] Some have even said that this (non-existent) curse of Ham resulted in the black "races."[37] This is absurd and is the type of false teaching that has reinforced and justified prejudices against people with dark skin.

In the genealogy in Matthew 1, it is traditionally understood that the same Rahab is listed here as being in the line leading to Christ. Thus, Rahab, a descendant of Ham, must have married an Israelite (descended from Shem). Since this was clearly a union approved by God, it underlines the fact that the particular "people group" she came from was irrelevant—what mattered was that she trusted in the true God of the Israelites.

The same can be said of Ruth, who as a Moabitess also married an Israelite and is also listed in the genealogy in Matthew 1 that leads to Christ. Prior to her marriage, she had expressed faith in the true God (Ruth 1:16).

When Rahab and Ruth became children of God, there was no longer any barrier to Israelites marrying them, even though they were from different people groups.

Real biblical "interracial" marriage

If one wants to use the term "interracial," then the real interracial marriage that God says we should not enter into is when a child of the Last Adam (one who is a new creation in Christ—a Christian) marries one who is an unconverted child of the First Adam (one who is dead in trespasses and sin—a non-Christian).[38]

Cross-cultural problems

Because many people groups have been separated since the Tower of Babel, they have developed many cultural differences. If two people from very different cultures marry, they can have a number of communication problems, even if both are Christians. Expectations regarding relationships with members of the extended family, for example, can also differ. Even people from different English-speaking countries can have communication problems because words may have different meanings. Counselors should go through this in detail, anticipating the problems and giving specific examples, as some marriages have failed because of such cultural differences. However, such problems have nothing to do with genetics or "race."

Conclusion

1. There is no biblical justification for claiming that people from different so-called races (best described as people groups) should not marry.

2. The biblical basis for marriage makes it clear that a Christian should marry only a Christian.

When Christians legalistically impose nonbiblical ideas, such as no interracial marriage onto their culture, they are helping to perpetuate prejudices that have often arisen from evolutionary influences. If we are really honest, in countries like America, the main reason for Christians being against interracial marriage is, in most instances, really because of skin color.

The church could greatly relieve the tensions over racism (particularly in countries like America), if only the leaders would teach biblical truths about our shared ancestry: all people are descended from one man and woman; all people are equal before God; all are sinners in need of salvation; all need to build their thinking on God's Word and judge all their cultural aspects accordingly; all need to be one in Christ and put an end to their rebellion against their Creator.

Christians must think about marriage as God thinks about each one of us. When the prophet Samuel went to anoint the next king of Israel, he thought the oldest of Jesse's sons was the obvious choice due to his outward appearance. However, we read in 1 Samuel 16:7, "But the Lord said to Samuel, 'Do not look at his appearance or at his physical stature, because I have refused him. For the Lord does not see as man sees; for man looks at the outward appearance, but the Lord looks at the heart.'" God doesn't look at our outward biological appearance; He looks on our inward spiritual state. And when considering marriage, couples should look on the inside spiritual condition of themselves and each other because it is true that what's on the inside, spiritually, is what really matters.

1.   J.P. Rushton, professor of psychology at the University of Western Ontario, Lond, Ontario, Canada, "Race, Evolution and Behavior," www.harbornet.com/folks/theedrich/JP_Rushton/Race.htm.

2.   S.J. Gould, *Ontogeny and Phylogeny* (Cambridge, MA: Belknap-Harvard Press, 1977), pp. 127–128.

3.   "Missing Links with Mankind in Early Dawn of History," *New York Tribune*, p. 11, February 10, 1924.

4.   D. Monaghan, "The Body-Snatchers," *The Bulletin*, November 12, 1991, pp. 30–38; "Blacks Slain for Science's White Superiority Theory, *The Daily Telegraph Mirror*, April 26, 1994.

5.   For more information on the fallacious nature of this idea, see www.answersingenesis.org/go/embryonic.

6.   Ernest Haeckel, *The History of Creation* (London: Henry S. King & Co., 1876), p. 363.

7.   Jerry Bergman, "Ota Benga: The Man Who Was Put on Display in the Zoo!" *Creation* December–February 1993, pp. 48–50.

8.   A.H.J. Keane, "Anthropological Curiosities; The Pygmies of the World," *Scientific American*, Supplement 1650, 64 no. 99 (1907): 107–108.

9.   This is not to say that *evolution* is the cause of racism. *Sin* is the cause of racism. However, Darwinian evolution fueled a particular form of racism.

10.   R.L. Hotz, "Race Has No Basis in Biology, Researchers Say," *Cincinnati Enquirer*, p. A3, February 20, 1997.

11.   ABC News, "We're All the Same," September 10, 1998, www.abcnews.com/sections/science/ DyeHard/dye72.html.

12.   S.C. Cameron and S.M. Wycoff, "The Destructive Nature of the Term Race: Growing Beyond a False Paradigm," *Journal of Counseling & Development* 76 (1998): 277–285.

13.   N. Angier, "Do Races Differ? Not Really, DNA Shows," *New York Times* web, Aug. 22, 2000.

14.   In the original, Ezra 9:2 refers to "seed," Romans 9:3 to "kinsmen according to the flesh."

15.   For more on this teaching, see chapter 6, Ken Ham, ed., *The New Answers Book 1* (Green Forest, AR: Master Books, 2006).

16.   Contrary to popular belief, mankind does not share an apelike ancestor with other primates. To find out the truth behind the alleged apemen, visit www.answersingenesis.org/go/anthropology.

17.   W.C. Kaiser, Jr. et al., *Hard Sayings of the Bible* (Downers Grove, IL: InterVarsity Press, 1996), p. 150.

18. Ibid., p. 644.

19. J.C. Gutin, "End of the Rainbow," *Discover*, November 1994, pp. 72–73.

20. S.C. Cameron and S.M. Wycoff, *Journal of Counseling & Development*.

21. N. Angier, *New York Times*.

22. ABC News, "We're All the Same."

23. Ibid.

24. Of course, melanin is not the only factor that determines skin shade: blood vessels close to the skin can produce a reddish tinge, while extra layers of adipose tissue (fat) in the skin yield a yellowish tinge. Exposure to the sun can cause increased melanin production, thus darkening skin, but only to a certain point. Other pigments also affect skin shade but generally have very little bearing on how light or dark the skin will be. The major provider of skin color is melanin.

25. Ackerman, *Histopathologic Diagnosis of Skin Diseases* (Philadelphia: Lea & Febiger, 1978), p. 44; Lever and Schamberg-Lever, *Histopathology of the Skin*, 7th Ed., (Philadelphia: J.B. Lippincott, 1990), pp. 18–20.

26. The actual genetics involved are much more complicated than this simplified explanation. There are 4 to 6 genes with multiples alleles (versions) of each gene that operate under incomplete dominance, that is, they work together to produce an individual's particular skin shade. However, simplifying the explanation does not take away from the point being made.

27. Albinism results from a genetic mutation which prevents the usual production of melanin.

28. For more information, see www.answersingenesis.org/go/red-hair.

29. As they went, the family groups took with them the knowledge that had been passed to them about the creation and Flood events. Although these accounts have been changed over time, they reflect the true account found in the Bible. For more information, see www.answersingenesis.org/go/legends.

30. This assumes that each trait is independently inherited, which may not always be the case. Although there are many instances in which a certain trait shows up in a person of a different ethnic group (e.g., almond-shaped eyes in a woman with very dark skin, or blue eyes in a man with tightly curled brown hair and tan skin).

31. For more on how selection and mutations operate, see chapter 22, Ken Ham, ed., *The New Answers Book 1* (Green Forest, AR; Master Books, 2006).

32. "Melanin," http://en.wikipedia.org/wiki/Melanin.

33. See note on Acts 17:26, in John Gill, D.D., *An exposition of the Old and New Testament*, London: printed for Mathews and Leigh, 18 Strand, by W. Clowes, Northumberland-Court, 1809. Edited, revised, and updated by Larry Pierce, 1994–1995 for Online Bible CD-ROM.

34. It is true that in some exceptional instances when a Christian has married a non-Christian, the non-Christian spouse, by the grace of God, has become a Christian. This is a praise point but it does not negate the fact that Scripture indicates that it should not have been entered into in the first place. This does not mean that the marriage is not actually valid, nor does it dilute the responsibilities of the marital union—see also 1 Corinthians 7:12–14, where the context is of one spouse becoming a Christian after marriage.

35. For more on this topic, see *Raising Godly Children in an Ungodly World* by Ken Ham and Steve Ham, available from www.answersbookstore.com.

36. See Genesis 9:18–27. Canaan, the youngest of Ham's sons, received Noah's curse. Why? The descendants of Canaan were some of the wickedest people on earth. For example, the people of Sodom and Gomorrah were judged for their sexual immorality and rebellion. It may be that Ham's actions toward his father (Genesis 9:22) had sexual connotations,

and Noah saw this same sin problem in Canaan and understood that Canaan's descendants would also act in these sinful ways. (The Bible clearly teaches that the unconfessed sin of one generation is often greater in the next generation.) The curse on Canaan has nothing to do with skin color but rather serves as a warning to fathers to train their children in the nurture and admonition of the Lord. We need to deal with our own sin problems and train our children to deal with theirs.

37. For example: "We know the circumstances under which the posterity of Cain (and later of Ham) were cursed with what we call Negroid racial characteristics" (Bruce McConkie, Apostle of the Mormon Council of 12, *Mormon Doctrine*, p. 554, 1958); "The curse which Noah pronounced upon Canaan was the origin of the black race" (The Golden Age, *The Watchtower* [now called *Awake!*], p. 702, July 24, 1929).

38. Examples of such "mixed marriages" and their negative consequences can be seen in Nehemiah 9, 10, and Numbers 25.

Ken Ham is President and CEO of Answers in Genesis–USA and the Creation Museum. Ken's bachelor's degree in applied science (with an emphasis on environmental biology) was awarded by the Queensland Institute of Technology in Australia. He also holds a diploma of education from the University of Queensland. In recognition of the contribution Ken has made to the church in the USA and internationally, Ken has been awarded two honorary doctorates: a Doctor of Divinity (1997) from Temple Baptist College in Cincinnati, Ohio and a Doctor of Literature (2004) from Liberty University in Lynchburg, Virginia.

Ken has authored or co-authored many books concerning the authority and accuracy of God's Word and the effects of evolutionary thinking, including *Genesis of a Legacy* and *The Lie: Evolution*.

Since moving to America in 1987, Ken has become one of the most in-demand Christian conference speakers and talk show guests in America. He has appeared on national shows such as Fox's *The O'Reilly Factor* and *Fox and Friends in the Morning*; CNN's *The Situation Room with Wolf Blitzer*, ABC's *Good Morning America*, the BBC, *CBS News Sunday Morning*, *The NBC Nightly News with Brian Williams*, and *The PBS News Hour with Jim Lehrer*.

William Wilberforce led Parliament in abolishing the slave trade throughout the British Empire. One month before all slaves in the British Empire were freed, William Wilberforce passed away.

Wilberforce: A Leader for Biblical Equality

by Paul F. Taylor

Many people believe the abolition of slavery began in the United States during the American Civil War of the 1860s. In fact, the abolitionist movement began decades earlier in the British Empire under the unrelenting leadership of one man, William Wilberforce.

William Wilberforce was born in 1759 in the English city of Kingston-upon-Hull. He was educated at St. John's College, Cambridge, and was elected as Hull's Member of Parliament in 1780.

Wilberforce became a Christian in 1784. His salvation drove him to consider deeply his position in politics, even to the point that he considered leaving politics to become a minister. He eventually concluded that God had called him to public office to further causes that were in line with biblical truth. The most famous of these causes was his commitment to abolish slavery. Wilberforce's salvation, therefore, had a profound influence on the history and way of life in the United Kingdom, the British Empire, and indirectly even the United States and its territories.

The Society for the Abolition of the Slave Trade was founded in May 1787. Support for the movement was nationwide but was particularly strong in Northern England.

In 1788 one hundred petitions attacking the slave trade went before the House of Commons, and in 1792 that political body voted in favor of the principle of abolition, 230 votes to 85. However, upon seeing the extreme radicalism of the French

Revolution, the Commons reversed the 1792 vote in 1793 hoping to avoid such a revolution in the British Empire.

Wilberforce and the other abolitionists were driven by their belief in the inerrancy of Scripture, acknowledging that God had made all nations of one blood (Acts 17:26) and that all men were created in the image of their Creator God (Genesis 1:26). John Wesley described slavery as "execrable villainy," and said, "Unless God has raised you up for this very thing [abolition], you will be worn out by the opposition of men and devils. But if God be for you who can stand against you?"[1]

Wilberforce's opponents included Lord Nelson, who later became the hero of the Battle of Trafalgar. Nelson wrote about the "damnable doctrine of Wilberforce and his hypocritical allies."[2] Wilberforce was known to be an abolitionist, but his strategy was first to end the slave trade. The Abolition of the Slave Trade Bill, which made the buying and selling of humans illegal throughout the British Empire and its colonies, became law on March 25, 1807.

Even with this success, Wilberforce was unfinished. He sought to see slavery completely abolished, believing that all people are descended from Adam and that none were less than human. At congresses in 1814 and 1815, held in Paris and Vienna

Britain's Parliament is where William Wilberforce struggled for man's equality before God, and where he fought to abolish the slave trade in the British Empire.

respectively, Wilberforce tried, unsuccessfully, to persuade other European powers to follow the abolitionist route.

Shortly before his death, Wilberforce learned that the Reform Act of 1833 had passed. Within four years that Act would outlaw all forms of slavery in the UK and the West Indies.

If slavery had not been abolished in the early nineteenth century under the influence of such Christians who understood the Bible's teaching on origins, what chance would there have been subsequently, as evolutionary thought took over in the mid-nineteenth century? Indeed, slavery has been retrospectively justified on the basis of the supposed lower order in the evolutionary process of certain "races." We can thank God for men like Wilberforce and the eighteenth-century Evangelical Awakening that brought so many souls to faith in Christ. Christians today should learn from Wilberforce's dedication to God's Word that the truths of God's Word, from the very first verse, should govern our standards. Wilberforce was guided by the truth that all men are descended from Adam, created in the image of God, and this truth continues to transform societies around the world.

1.   John Wesley's last letter, written to encourage William Wilberforce on February 24, 1791, cited on BBC website, www.bbc.co.uk/religion/religions/christianity/features/wilberforce/page6.shtml.

2.   Quoted from a letter written by Nelson from the flagship *Victory*, cited in *The Telegraph of London*, www.telegraph.co.uk/travel/main.jhtml?xml=/travel/2000/12/11/etfis11.xml.

Paul F. Taylor graduated with his BSc in chemistry from Nottingham University and his master's in science education from Cardiff University. Paul taught science for 17 years in a state school but is now a proficient writer and speaker for Answers in Genesis-UK.

How Should a Christian Respond to Gay Marriage?

by Ken Ham

What do the TV shows *ER*, *Will & Grace*, and *Desperate House-wives* have in common? They all portray homosexual behavior as a normal and acceptable lifestyle. Television sitcoms, network news, and our public education system bombard us with the message of tolerance for gays and lesbians. Many states are debating same-sex marriage initiatives, and the US Government is considering the Federal Marriage Amendment, which would define marriage as the union between a man and a woman only. What does the Bible say about gay marriage? How should a Christian respond to this issue? These are the questions we will tackle in this chapter as we learn how to think biblically about moral issues.

Most people have heard of the account of Adam and Eve. According to the first book of the Bible, Genesis, these two people were the first humans from whom all others in the human race descended. Genesis also records the names of three of Adam and Eve's many children—Cain, Abel, and Seth.

Christians claim that this account of human history is accurate, because the Bible itself claims that it is the authoritative Word of the Creator God, without error.

To challenge Christians' faith in the Bible as an infallible revelation from God to humans, many skeptics have challenged the Bible's trustworthiness as a historical document by asking questions like, "Where did Cain find his wife?" (Don't worry—this will become highly relevant to the topic of gay marriage shortly!)

This question of Cain's wife is one of the most-asked questions about the Christian faith and the Bible's reliability. In short, Genesis 5:4 states that Adam had "other sons and daughters"; thus, originally, brothers had to marry sisters.[1]

An atheist on a talk show

This background is helpful in offering the context of a conversation I had with a caller on a radio talk show. The conversation went something like this:

Caller: "I'm an atheist, and I want to tell you Christians that if you believe Cain married his sister, then that's immoral."

AiG: "If you're an atheist, then that means you don't believe in any personal God, right?"

Caller: "Correct!"

AiG: "Then if you don't believe in God, you don't believe there's such a thing as an absolute authority. Therefore, you believe everyone has a right to their own opinions—to make their own rules about life if they can get away with it, correct?"

Caller: "Yes, you're right."

AiG: "Then, sir, you can't call me immoral; after all, you're an atheist, who doesn't believe in any absolute authority."

The AiG guest went on: "Do you believe all humans evolved from apelike ancestors?"

Caller: "Yes, I certainly believe evolution is fact."

AiG: "Then, sir, from your perspective on life, if man is just some sort of animal who evolved, and if there's no absolute authority, then marriage is whatever you want to define it to be—if you can get away with it in the culture you live in.

"It could be two men, two women, or one man and ten women; in fact, it doesn't even have to be a man with another human—it could be a man with an animal.[2]

"I'm sorry, sir, that you think Christians have a problem. I think it's you who has the problem. Without an absolute authority, marriage, or any other aspect of how to live in society, is determined on the basis of opinion and ultimately could be anything one decides—if the culture as a whole will allow you to get away with this. You have the problem, not me."

It was a fascinating—and revealing—exchange.

So the question, then, that could be posed to this caller and other skeptics is this: "Who has the right to determine what is good or bad, or what is morally right or wrong in the culture? Who determines whether marriage as an institution should be adhered to, and if so, what the rules should be?"

The "pragmatics" aspect of opposing gay marriage—some cautions

Some who defend marriage as a union between one man and one woman claim that it can be shown that cultures that have not adhered to this doctrine have reaped all sorts of problems (whether the spread of diseases or other issues). Thus, they claim, on this basis, it's obvious that marriage should be between one man and one woman only.

Even though such problems as the spread of HIV might be shown to be a sound argument in this issue, ultimately it's not a good basis for stating that one man for one woman must be the rule. It may be a sound argument based on the pragmatics of wanting to maintain a healthy physical body, but why should one or more human beings have the right to dictate to others what they can or can't do in sexual relationships? After all, another person might decide that the relationship between one man and woman in marriage might cause psychological problems and use that as the basis for the argument. So which one is correct?

Say that a person used the argument that research has shown, for example, that the children of gay parents had a higher incidence of depression. Or the argument that since HIV kills people, it is vital that marriage is between a man and a woman. But note how such arguments have also been tried in the case of abortion and *rejected* by the culture.

Let us illustrate. Some researchers claim to have shown a high incidence of depression in people who have had an abortion. The culture, however, has rejected such pragmatic "we shouldn't hurt people" arguments, claiming that it is more important that others have the "right to choose." The argument that abortion kills people is an important one because most people still accept the basic biblical prohibition against taking innocent human life. So we should ensure that people know that the baby is really human. But is it going to be enough in the long term, as even this prohibition cannot be absolute without the Bible?

The morals of the majority

Over the centuries in our Western nations, people (including their leaders) almost universally accepted the belief that marriage was to be one man for one woman. In recent times, that once-prevailing view has been shifting—and rapidly.

What has brought about this change in the past few decades? The answer can be boiled down to how one considers this question: Who in society determines what is morally wrong or right? Years ago, for example, most Americans were not pro-abortion (or even "pro-choice") and did not want abortion legalized. But a moral absolute regarding the sanctity of life has been dramatically tossed aside in recent times, so much so that even politicians who might be morally conservative in many areas have now moved to a pro-choice position and will not raise an objection to a woman's "right to choose."

Over the years, as society's beliefs about absolute moral standards have changed concerning abortion and other issues, the laws have changed accordingly. So while the majority might agree on particular standards and laws today, they can be overturned by the next generation. What may appear to be absolute for one generation might not be absolute for another.

Increasingly, people are becoming more tolerant, not only of abortion but also of gay marriage. Given the abortion example above, what is to prevent a majority of society declaring one day that same-sex marriage is permissible? And then what about polygamy, or even pedophilia? Indeed, a shifting morality can be a slippery slope, to the point that one day society might determine that polygamy and sex between adults and children are not wrong—as long as most people believe that they are acceptable. Now, some might object and say that these now-illegal things would never be allowed in America. But who in the 1960s would have believed that America would one day allow abortions and see gay marriages performed?

Without an absolute moral standard, people are free to make up their own morals (and change them as the majority dictates). Should we be surprised when some Western nations will one day allow parents to kill their newborns because there might be a defect in the child? The majority might be lulled into sympathizing with the anguished parent, and also piously thinking something like: "Who wants to have a child go through life in that kind of condition?"

Does the church have the answer?

The gay marriage issue has been headline news across North America and on other continents. Even the acceptance of gay clergy has been widely noted in both secular and Christian media outlets.

- In November 2003 a part of the Episcopal Church voted to ordain a gay bishop. Thus, the world saw part of the church now condoning homosexual behavior.[3]

- On March 18, 2004, the Pacific Northwest Conference of the United Methodist Church in America supported a lesbian pastor. Once again, the world looked on as a large denomination legitimized homosexual behavior.[4]

As part of the public debate on the gay marriage issue, many church leaders have been interviewed on national TV programs and asked to share their position on this topic. While the majority of church leaders have been speaking against gay unions and have been defending marriage as being between one man and one woman, many of these same church leaders have not been able to adequately defend their position.

One Christian leader was interviewed on MSNBC-TV and was asked about the gay marriage issue. The interview went something like this:

TV host: "Did Jesus deal directly with the gay marriage issue?"

Christian leader: "No, but then Jesus didn't deal directly with the abortion issue or many other issues . . . ."

This is such a disappointing response. A proper response could have been such a powerful witness—not only to the interviewer but to the potential millions of viewers watching the news program, so people could understand why this Christian leader opposed gay marriage.

The same Christian leader appeared on CNN-TV doing an interview that, in part, went something like the following:

Interviewer: "Why are you against gay marriage?"

Christian leader: "Because down through the ages, culture after culture has taught that marriage is between a man and a woman."

We believe this kind of answer actually opens the door to gay marriage! How? Because it basically says that marriage is determined by law or opinion.

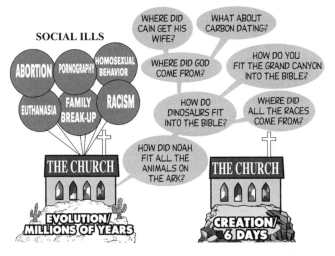

So, why is it that we don't see many Christian leaders giving the right sorts of answers? We think it's because the majority of them have compromised with the idea of millions of years of history, as well as evolutionary beliefs in astronomy, geology, and so on. As a result, the Bible's authority has been undermined, and it's no longer understood to be the absolute authority.[5]

Gay marriage—is evolution the cause?

After reading explanations from Answers in Genesis such as those above, some critics have concluded that we are saying that belief in millions of years or other evolutionary ideas is the cause of social ills like gay marriage. This is not true at all.

It is accurate to say that the increasing acceptance of homosexual behavior and gay marriage has gone hand in hand with the popularity and acceptance of millions of years and evolutionary ideas. But this does not mean that every person who believes in millions of years/evolution accepts gay marriage or condones homosexual behavior.

But the more people (whether Christian or not) believe in man's ideas concerning the history of the universe, the more man's fallible ideas are used as a basis for determining "truth" and overriding the Bible's authority.

People need to understand that homosexual behavior and the gay marriage controversy are ultimately not the problems in our culture, but are the symptoms of a much deeper problem. Even though it's obvious from the Bible that homosexual behavior and gay marriage are an abomination (Romans 1 and other passages make this very clear), there is a foundational reason as to why there is an increasing acceptance of these ills in America and societies like it.

What does the Bible say about homosexual behavior and gay marriage?

Study the following verses:

- Genesis 2:18–25
- Leviticus 18:22
- Mark 10:6
- Romans 1:26–27
- 1 Corinthians 6:9–10
- 1 Timothy 1:9–10

Cultures in the West were once pervaded by a primarily Christian worldview because the majority of people at least respected the Bible as the authority on morality.

It needs to be clearly understood that over the past two hundred years the Bible's authority has been increasingly undermined, as much of the church has compromised with the idea of millions of years (this began before Darwin) and has thus begun reinterpreting Genesis. When those outside the church saw church leaders rejecting Genesis as literal history, one can understand why they would have quickly lost respect for all of the Bible. If the church doesn't even believe this Book to be true, then why should the world build its morality on a fallible work that modern science supposedly has shown to be inaccurate in its science and history?

The Bible has lost respect in people's eyes (both within and without the church) to the extent that the culture as a whole now does not take the Bible's morality seriously at all. The increasing acceptance of homosexual behavior and gay marriage is a symptom of the loss of biblical authority, and is primarily due to the compromise the church has made with the secular world's teaching on origins.

Mocking the Bible

For example, consider the following. A New Orleans newspaper printed a commentary entitled, "In gay rights debate, Genesis is losing."[6] The column pointed out (correctly) that God intended marriage to be between one man and one woman. The writer even quoted Genesis 2:24, which declares, "Therefore shall a man leave his father and his mother and shall cleave to his wife: and they shall be one flesh."

The author then, mockingly, wrote, "Ah, Genesis. Heaven and earth created in six days, a serpent that talks and a 600-year-old man building an ark. Just the guide we need to set rational policy."

This secular writer recognized that the literal history of Genesis was the basis for the belief that marriage is one man for one woman.

However, by mocking the Genesis account (just as many church leaders effectively do when they reinterpret Genesis 1–11 on the basis of man's fallible ideas), the writer removed the foundations upon which the institution of marriage stands. This opens the door to gay marriage or anything else one might determine about marriage.

Are people born to a homosexual lifestyle?

We won't presume to offer a definitive answer as to what causes homosexual behavior. We can point out, however, that in a world that has experienced over 6,000 years of the Curse (Genesis 3), it is not difficult to argue that genetic factors accumulated over the millennia could lead to a predisposition toward aberrant behavior. And, of course, there is the combined factor of personal choice involved, where people who are inclined toward a certain behavior can decide whether or not to follow through on a course of action. In other words, a person's lifestyle can be influenced by that individual's genetic makeup (and perhaps even by how that person was brought up—nature plus nurture).

In fact, Christian behavioral researchers point out, for example, that some people can be more genetically predisposed to alcoholism, to committing violent acts, etc. Now, this does not mean that these actions are to be condoned (the Bible calls them sin), because a predisposition does not lead a potential alcoholic to automatically walk into a bar to begin his drinking habit. Intentional, personal choice can certainly fend off that predisposition. While all people sin (Romans 3 and Romans 6) and thus that it is "natural," it does not make the sinning correct or acceptable.

Therefore, even if some genetic component (a so-called "homosexual gene" as some might call it) were found, it does not make this sin natural or normal. As indicated before, this world suffers from thousands of years of the Curse, and in this fallen, decaying world, all kinds of genetic mistakes have been occurring. It is important to note that such abnormalities are the result of the Curse, not of any creation by the Creator. Moreover, what Scripture teaches against certain behavior (drunkenness, infidelity, homosexual behavior, etc.) trumps what anyone might say is acceptable behavior. There is right and wrong apart from people's opinions of what they might observe in nature and what it suggests to them, and that moral standard comes from God's Word.

It is possible that how a child grows up in certain situations might play a factor in determining sexual identity. Thankfully, though, the Bible presents all kinds of teaching on how to correctly raise children. Sadly, though, it may not be far-fetched to say that as the breakdown of the family continues in America and as people increasingly reject biblical principles, impressionable young people will be even more inclined toward homosexuality, and thus gay marriage will probably grow. However, standing up for biblical truths in the culture can stem that tide.

Gay marriage—what is the answer?

In the Bible's book of Judges 17:6, we read this statement: "When they had no king to tell them what to do, they all did what was right in their own eyes." In other words, when there's no absolute authority to decide right and wrong, everyone has their own opinion as to what they should do.

So how could the Christian leader whose interviews were quoted earlier in this chapter have responded differently? Well, consider this answer:

First of all, Jesus (who created us and therefore owns us and has the authority to determine right and wrong), as the God-man, *did* deal directly with the gay marriage issue, in the Bible's New Testament, in Matthew 19:4–6:

"And He answered and said to them, 'Have you not read that He who made them at the beginning "made them male and female," and said, "For this reason a man shall leave his father and mother and be joined to his wife, and the two shall become one flesh?" So then, they are no longer two but one flesh. Therefore what God has joined together, let not man separate."'

He could have continued:

Christ quoted directly from the book of Genesis (and its account of the creation of Adam and Eve as the first man and woman—the first marriage) as literal history, to explain the doctrine of marriage as being one man for one woman. Thus marriage cannot be a man and a man, or a woman and a woman.

Because Genesis is real history (as can be confirmed by observational science, incidentally), Jesus dealt quite directly with the gay marriage issue when he explained the doctrine of marriage.

Not only this, but in John 1 we read:

"In the beginning was the Word, and the Word was with God, and the Word was God. The same was in the beginning with God. All things were made by him; and without him was not any thing made that was made."

Jesus, the Creator, is the Word. The Bible is the written Word. Every word in the Bible is really the Word of the Creator—Jesus Christ.[7]

Therefore, in Leviticus 18:22, Jesus deals directly with the homosexual issue, and thus the gay marriage issue. This is also true of Romans 1:26–27 and 1 Timothy 1:9–10.

Because Jesus in a real sense wrote all of the Bible, whenever Scripture deals with marriage and/or the homosexual issue, Jesus Himself is directly dealing with these issues.

Even in a secular context, the only answer a Christian

should offer is this:

The Bible is the Word of our Creator, and Genesis is literal history. Its science and history can be trusted. Therefore, we have an absolute authority that determines marriage.

God made the first man and woman—the first marriage. Thus, marriage can only be a man and a woman because we are accountable to the One who made marriage in the first place.

And don't forget—according to Scripture, one of the primary reasons for marriage is to produce godly offspring.[8] Adam and Eve were told to be fruitful and multiply, but there's no way a gay marriage can fulfill this command!

The battle against gay marriage will ultimately be lost (like the battle against abortion) *unless* the church and the culture return to the absolute authority beginning in Genesis. Then and only then will there be a true foundation for the correct doctrine of marriage—one man for one woman for life.

---

1. For a more detailed answer to this question, see www.AnswersInGenesis.org/go/cains-wife.

2. See "Man Marries Dog for Luck—Then Dies," *The Age*, http://www.the age.com.au/articles2004/02/04/1075853937098.html; and M. Bates "Marriage in the New Millennium: Love, Honor and Scratch Between the Ears," *Oak Lawn (Illinois) Reporter*, April 5, 2001, as referenced at http://www. freerepublic.com/forum/a3ac9e00d0a87.htm. There are many articles online that discuss the possibility of a man marrying his dog if the sanctity of marriage is not upheld; search for words like *marriage, man* and *dog*.

3. "Episcopal Church Consecrates Openly Gay Bishop," CNN.com, November 3, 2003.

4. Read the church proceedings for and against Rev. Karen Dammann at http://www.pnwumc.org/Dammann.htm.

5. For more information on this important point, see chapter 6, Ken Ham, ed., *The New Answers Book 2* (Green Forest, AR; Master Books, 2008).

6. J. Gill, *Times-Picayune*, New Orleans, March 5, 2004.

7. See Colossians 1:15–20 as well.

8. Malachi 2:15: "Has not the Lord made them one? In flesh and spirit they are his. And why one? Because he was seeking godly offspring. So guard yourself in your spirit, and do not break faith with the wife of your youth."

Evolution and the Challenge of Morality

by Jason Lisle

Morality is a very difficult problem for the evolutionary worldview. This isn't to say that evolutionists are somehow less moral than anyone else. Most of them adhere to a code of behavior. Like the biblical creationist, they do believe in the concepts of *right* and *wrong*. The problem is that evolutionists have no logical reason to believe in right and wrong within their own worldview. Right and wrong are Christian concepts which go back to Genesis. By attempting to be moral, therefore, the evolutionist is being irrational; for he must borrow biblical concepts which are contrary to his worldview.

The genesis of morality

The Bible teaches that God is the Creator of all things (Genesis 1:1; John 1:3). All things belong to God (Psalm 24:1) and thus, God has the right to make the rules. So, an absolute moral code makes sense in a biblical creation worldview. But if the Bible were not true, if human beings were merely the outworking of millions of years of mindless chemical processes, then why should we hold to a universal code of behavior? Could there really be such concepts as right and wrong if evolution were true?

Evolutionary "morality"

Some might respond, "Well, I believe in right and wrong, and I also believe in evolution; so, obviously they can go together."

But this does not follow. People can be irrational; they can profess to believe in things that are contrary to each other. The question is not about what people believe to be the case, but rather what actually is the case. Can the concepts of right and wrong really be meaningful apart from the biblical God? To put it another way, is morality *justified* in an evolutionary worldview?

In response to this, an evolutionist might say, "Of course. People can create their own moral code apart from God. They can adopt their own standards of right and wrong." However, this kind of thinking is arbitrary, and will lead to absurd consequences. If everyone can create his or her own morality, then no one could argue that what *other* people do is actually wrong, since other people can also invent their own personal moral code. For example, a person might choose for himself a moral code in which murder is perfectly acceptable. This might seem upsetting to us, but how could we argue that it is wrong *for others* to murder if morality is nothing but a personal standard? If morality is a subjective personal choice, then Hitler cannot be denounced for his actions, since he was acting in accord with his chosen standard. Clearly this is an unacceptable position.

Some evolutionists argue that there *is* an absolute standard; they say, "Right is what brings the most happiness to the most people." But this is also arbitrary. Why should *that* be the selected standard as opposed to some other view? Also, notice that this view borrows from the Christian position. In the Christian worldview, we should indeed be concerned about the happiness of others since they are made in God's image.[1] But if other people are simply chemical accidents, why should we care about their happiness at all? Concern about others does not make sense in an evolutionary universe.

Perhaps, the evolutionist will claim that morality is what the majority decides it to be. But this view has the same defects as the others. It merely shifts an unjustified opinion from one person to a group of people. It is arbitrary and leads to absurd conclusions. Again, we find that we would not be able to denounce certain actions that we know to be wrong. After all, Hitler was able to convince a majority of his people that his actions were right, but that doesn't really make them right.

Without the biblical God, *right* and *wrong* are reduced to mere personal preferences. In an evolutionary universe, the statement "murder is wrong" is nothing more than a personal opinion on the same level as "blue is my favorite color." And if others have a different opinion, we would have no basis for arguing with them. Thus, when evolutionists talk about morality as if it is a real standard that other people should follow, they are being inconsistent with their own worldview.

Evolutionary inconsistency

As one example, consider those evolutionists who are very concerned about children being taught creation. "This is wrong," they say, "because you're lying to children!" Now, obviously this begs the question, since the truth or falsity of creation is the concern at issue: we are convinced that creation is true, and evolution is the lie. But the truly absurd thing about such evolutionary arguments is that they are contrary to evolution! That is, in an evolutionary worldview why shouldn't we lie—particularly if it benefits our survival value?

Now certainly the Christian believes that it's wrong to lie, but then again, the Christian has a reason for this. God has indicated in His Word that lying is contrary to His nature (Numbers 23:19), and that we are not to engage in it (Exodus 20:16). But apart from the biblical worldview, why *should* we tell the truth? For that matter, why should we do anything at all? Words like *should* and *ought* only make sense if there is an absolute standard given by one who has authority over everyone.

If human beings are merely chemical accidents, why should we be so concerned about what they do? We wouldn't get mad at baking soda for reacting with vinegar; that's just what chemicals do. So, why would an evolutionist be angry at anything one human being does to another, if we are all nothing more than complex chemical reactions? If we are simply evolved animals, why should we hold to a code of conduct in this "dog-eat-dog" world? After all, what one animal does to another is morally irrelevant. When evolutionists attempt to be moral, they are "borrowing" from the Christian worldview.

Evolutionists must borrow morality from the biblical worldview

One humorous example of this happened at the opening of the Creation Museum. A group opposing the museum had hired a plane to circle above with a trailing banner that read, "Defcon says: Thou shalt not lie." Of course, we couldn't agree more! After all, this is one of the Ten Commandments. In fact, the purpose of the Creation Museum is to present the truth about origins. So, the evolutionists had to borrow from the biblical worldview in order to argue against it. In an evolutionary universe, Defcon's moral objection makes no sense (although we certainly appreciated the free advertising).

Making sense of the evolutionary position

The Christian worldview not only accounts for morality, but it also accounts for why evolutionists behave the way they do. Even those who have no basis for morality within their own professed worldview nonetheless hold to a moral code; this is because in their heart of hearts, they really do know the God of creation—despite their profession to the contrary. Scripture tells us that everyone knows the biblical God, but that they suppress the truth about God. (Romans 1:18–21). Why would anyone do this?

We have inherited a sin nature (a tendency to rebel against God) from Adam (Romans 5:12), who rebelled against God in the Garden of Eden (Genesis 3). John 3:19 indicates that people would rather remain in spiritual darkness than have their evil deeds exposed. Just as Adam tried to hide from God's presence (Genesis 3:8), so his descendents do the same. But the solution to sin is not suppression, it is confession and repentance (1 John 1:9; Luke 5:32). Christ is faithful to forgive anyone who calls on His name (Romans 10:13).

Conclusions

Nearly everyone believes that people ought to behave in a certain way—a moral code. Yet, in order for morality to be meaningful, biblical creation must be true. Since God created human beings, He determines what is to be considered *right* and *wrong*, and we are responsible to Him for our actions. We must therefore conclude that evolutionists are being irrational when they talk about right and wrong, for such concepts make no sense in an evolutionary universe.

---

1. The happiness of others, though important, is not the primary concern within the Christian worldview. To love, obey, and glorify the God who has created and saved us should be our primary focus (Mark 12:30; Ecclesiastes 12:13). One aspect of this is that we should treat others with love and respect (Matthew 7:12; Mark 12:31).

Jason Lisle earned his PhD in astrophysics from the University of Colorado at Boulder. As one of the few creationist astrophysicists doing research today, he works full-time in AiG's new Research Division. He also programs and designs the shows for the Creation Museum's Stargazers Room planetarium.

Right or Wrong?

You may not have thought much about it, but how do you know what is right and what is wrong? Different cultures have different standards, but there is an underlying sense of morality in all people. Everyone has a conscience! No matter where you go, people know that it is wrong to steal, to lie, and to murder. Evolutionary scientists try to explain this as a response that has helped groups of people survive over millions of years. This story helps explain what they think may have happened, but there is no way to test if it is true. In fact, if humans are simply highly evolved apes, why is it wrong to murder or steal or lie? If it helps an individual to survive and pass on their genes, it should be applauded to be consistent with an evolutionary worldview.

That feeling that you get when you lie, cheat, or steal comes from your conscience. Rather than being the result of random chemical reactions that were shaped by evolutionary processes, your conscience is given to you by God. If there is a moral law, there must be a moral Lawgiver. In the Bible, we read that everyone shows "the work of the law written in their hearts, their conscience also bearing witness, and between themselves their thoughts accusing or else excusing them" (Romans 2:15). Everyone knows what is right and wrong because God has given each person a knowledge of right and wrong—the conscience.

Even though those who commit these crimes know they are wrong, they suppress that truth and bring the judgment of God upon themselves:

> For the wrath of God is revealed from heaven against

all ungodliness and unrighteousness of men, who suppress the truth in unrighteousness, because what may be known of God is manifest in them, for God has shown it to them. For since the creation of the world His invisible attributes are clearly seen, being understood by the things that are made, even His eternal power and Godhead, so that they are without excuse, because, although they knew God, they did not glorify Him as God, nor were thankful, but became futile in their thoughts, and their foolish hearts were darkened (Romans 1:18–21).

There are no true atheists, only those who choose to reject God. God has revealed His law in the hearts of all men (the conscience) but He has also revealed it in His written word—the Bible. In the Bible you can find what God demands of mankind. He has the right to make these demands because He is the Creator of the universe. The first chapters of the book of Genesis describe how God created the universe and the first man and woman. He gave them a single command and they chose to eat of the forbidden fruit. This was the first sin committed by mankind—and sin has been with us ever since.

Every time that we break one of God's commands we are sinning. God is described as a just Judge (Psalm 7:11), and so He must punish those who break His laws. Would you be guilty if God judged you against His holy standard? Does your conscience confirm your guilt? If you have ever told a lie, stolen anything (no matter the value), put anything before God, or used His name in a loose way, you have sinned against God. These things may seem somewhat trivial to you, and you may think you will be excused since everyone else has done these things, too. Regardless of how you feel, however, you stand condemned before the God of the universe.

But all is not lost. You still have hope in avoiding the consequences of your actions. Not only is God just, He is also merciful.

In His mercy, He orchestrated a plan that would rescue sinners. Jesus Christ, God in the flesh, stepped into His creation so that He could pay the penalty for the sins of mankind. He lived a perfect life—did not commit a single sin—and then offered Himself as a substitute for the penalty that each person deserves. As He hung on the Cross, God poured out His wrath against sin on Jesus. This substitutionary sacrifice is made available for all of those who will repent of their sins, confess them to God, and turn from that sin as they trust in Christ's death to save them.

This is the message of the gospel. The Bible gives the true history of the earth and mankind. Not only does it reveal the past, but it reveals what will happen in the future. After Jesus died on the Cross, He was buried and rose to life on the third day, demonstrating His power over death (1 Corinthians 15:3–6). Christ will return to the earth one day, and each man will be judged for his sins. Those who belong to Christ will be resurrected to eternal life in heaven; those who do not will spend an eternity separated from God in hell.

As you examine your life, does your conscience scream, "Guilty!"? The Bible tells us that there is salvation in no other name besides Jesus Christ (Acts 4:12). Many people try to suppress their consciences with a busy lifestyle, drugs and alcohol, or by simply rejecting God and putting something else in His rightful place in their lives.

When you stand before God, how will you answer for your sins? Will you allow Christ to be your Lord and Savior, or will you reject His kind offer of salvation?

A POCKET GUIDE TO . . .

Social Issues

What does the Bible say about morality?

WHEN DOES LIFE BEGIN? • PLANNED PARENTHOOD • CLONING •
RE THERE REALLY DIFFERENT RACES? • HOW SHOULD A CHRISTIAN
RESPOND TO GAY MARRIAGE? • THE CHALLENGE OF MORALITY